Our Michigan
Ethnic Tales & Recipes

Edited by
Carole Eberly

Cover by TONI GORKIN

Illustrations by BEVERLY WOODARD

eberly press

1004 Michigan Ave.
East Lansing, MI 48823

ISBN 0-932296-03-3

Thanks

It's impossible to mention all the people who helped make this book possible. But I do owe special thanks to the people at the Michigan State Library for letting me check out bushels of material at a time, then letting me keep it weeks beyond the due dates without sending the sheriff after me.

Also, thanks to my fellow freelancing friend, Judy Eldridge, the people at the Peter White Public Library in Marquette, David Johnson at the State Photo Archives, Mary Flachsenhaar of the Detroit Free Press, Evelyn Cairns of the Mellus Newspapers and Christine Kolassa of St. Marys Rosary Society in Bronson.

Eat, Eat, Eat!

It's been my destiny to do this book ever since I was an infant and first heard my Czech grandmother speak her favorite American words, "Eat, eat, eat."

Sunday dinner at her home in Dearborn was a feast. There I would sit, perched on the Detroit phone directory as a make-shift booster chair, facing mounds of stewed chicken and dumplings or veal paprikash or creamed kidneys or stuffed green peppers or homemade noodles swimming in butter. Of course there was her 10,000-calorie rolled nut bread to accompany all this.

And no one dared decline seconds or thirds on anything. After all, we couldn't insult grandma. Besides, how did you expect to grow up to be big and strong — or just plain big and fat?

Since grandma had ten children, she never lacked for company on weekends. Aunts, uncles, nieces, nephews, cousins, friends — we'd all pile in on her awaiting the banquet. I can't recall less than twelve persons ever sitting around the dining room table stuffing themselves.

Grandma never sat down for dinner. She was too busy feeding everyone else. She ate afterwards, when she said she could relax — content, perhaps, with the thought everyone had been properly stuffed and lay moaning in the living room chairs.

Grandma was a cook at mountain resorts in the old country, so she knew what she was doing in the kitchen; and she liked an appreciative audience.

Although my grandma told me stories of her in the old country and coming over here as a young woman working as a governess in New York, I never cared much about listening. Unfortunately, I was too young and too American to recognize the value of those stories. Her life, to me, was light years removed from mine.

I was thirteen when she died, taking many of those stories with her. How I wish she were here today.

I never learned to speak Czech. My parents spoke it when they didn't want my brother or me to know what they were talking about — mainly us. The only thing I learned was from my grandma — "I'm hungry." She said that was all I'd ever have to know to get by in life.

My family, like many other families of immigrants, was too busy fitting into the American groove to carry on many Czech traditions and customs — except for cooking. My mother has taught me grandma's cooking (can a plastic and steel Cuisinart compare to a time-weathered chopping block and hand kneading?), they're passable.

Cooking is the one link that remains with many of my generation and their grandparents or beyond.

But while cooking is important and great, there are stories unique to each group in America. In compiling this book I decided to find some of these stories — to use interviews, first person accounts, historical pieces and thumbnail sketches to give readers a glimpse at each group. The accounts are by no means complete looks at each group, nor are they even representative of it. They simply tell a story involving that particular ethnic group.

I know right now I'm going to hear from those groups that aren't included in the book. (And, having spent my teenage years in Sao Paulo, Brazil and Mexico City you'd think I'd have something on the Latinos and Mexican-Americans, right?) Well, I had to stop somewhere. Also, I used those groups where material was accessible and interesting. Everyone has a story to tell, but unless it was at the State Library or sent to me, I didn't find it.

However, if you have some material that would look good in an anthology, get in touch with me. If I collect enough, I'll do Volume II, or "Son of Our Michigan" — or something.

And so, read on. And eat, eat, eat!

— Carole Eberly

Table of Contents

When Grandfather Julius Came to Michigan

"I would never permit my children to jump logs." These words from my father were my introduction to Michigan history. They recalled his youth when there was an active lumber business in the rivers. My father and his teen-aged friends "jumped logs" for the sport of it as they floated down the Boardman River to the saw mills in Traverse City. Youth wanted to 'live dangerously' in those days too.

Grandfather Julius Steinberg came to Traverse City in 1868 at the age of twenty-one. He came from Suwalk, Russia (Russian Poland). Remaining behind, until he could send for them, were his young wife, Mary, and their infant son, Jacob, my father. His departure had been hurried as military conscription into the Czar's army threatened his plan to come to the New World. Leaving was a problem. He solved it by escaping disguised in women's clothes. His brother accompanied him to the border, overcame the border police officer, thus making the escape possible. Under the corrupt goverment of the Czar, police officers did not report their failures. At a safe distance on the other side Julius shed the women's clothes and went to an inn. His troubles were not over. The innkeeper asked to see his passport. Nothing daunted, Julius showed him a luach (Hebrew calendar). The innkeeper, like most people in those days, could not read. He left with the luach to get confirmation that it was a passport. Meanwhile, a Jewish man in the inn helpfully showed Julius out the back door. Julius made his way to England where he worked to earn his passage money to America and learned a little English.

We do not know what brought Grandfather Julius to Traverse City, a settlement that was not yet a village (Traverse City was incorporated as a village in 1881 and as a city in 1895. The first settlers came to Traverse City in 1847-9 following a Mr. Boardman

By Devera Steinberg Stocker

Reprinted with permission from the "Michigan Jewish History Magazine," Nov. 1965.

9

who set up a saw mill in 1847.). The main industry was lumbering though agriculture was beginning to make progress. He made his living as a peddler, carrying his stock of wares to the farmers. Peddlers were welcome in those days. This was the way the early settlers secured and replenished their needs. Grandfather Julius had a lively sense of humor. One of his hurdles he told us was learning the English language. In the early days of his struggle he learned that 'please' was a nice word. He used it, therefore, at every opportunity even adding it to his greetings —"hello, please" and "goodbye, please." As a child I could imagine Grandfather Julius trudging through the snow with his pack, very tired, but greeting the farmer with a cheerful "hello, please." He preceded his jokes with a little laugh, a delightful characteristic which gave him our attention in anticipation of what was to follow.

He made progress, soon graduating to carrying his wares by horse and wagon and later setting up a dry goods store in a permanent location. Meanwhile he had sent for his wife and son. They arrived in this country approximately in September of 1871. On October 8th, 1871 he returned to Traverse City from Chicago where he had left his wife and child for a visit with their "landsleit" friends, the Bernsteins. From the boat he could see the flames of the now famous Chicago fire. One of his daughters, Ella, married Meyer Bernstein, son of his good friends.

Together Julius and Mary established the store and raised their seven children: Jacob ("Jake"), Kate, Alec, Ella, Irene, Birde and Leon. A newspaper advertisement, approximately 1890, gives us an idea of the merchandise carried: The Reliable Dry Goods, Carpet & Clothing House of Julius Steinberg, Ladies and Gents' Furnishing Goods, Hats & Caps, Trunks & Valises." The store remained under the family name for more than fifty years. With time it became Julius Steinberg and Sons, later Steinberg Bros., when Jake and Alec took over, and finally the J. H. Steinberg Store until Jake's death in 1922.

In 1891 Grandfather Julius built Steinberg's Grand Opera House. From *THE GRAND TRAVERSE HERALD*, December 13, 1894, comes this description: "The opening of Steinberg's Grand Opera House Tuesday evening was one of the greatest successes and most brilliant social events that Traverse City has ever known, and Mr. Steinberg is kept busy receiving congratulations upon his enterprise in erecting so fine a building and securing for the opening night so eminent a tragedian as Walker Whiteside." A detailed description followed. For many years stock companies played there until the advent of the cinema. It became one of the important theatrical centers in Northern Michigan. Among the later famous names who played there were Walker Whiteside, May Robeson, Eva Tanguay, Mack Sennett, Wm. S. Hart, and Fred Stone.

With the coming of the cinema, movies were shown for a short time. This was terminated in 1915 when a law was passed in Michigan forbidding the showing of movies in second floor theaters because of fire hazard. Again, nothing daunted, Julius built a movie theater, The Lyric, next door to the store (The Lyric, under a new name, still serves movie goers in Traverse City. It was remodeled and the name changed to the State Theater in approximately 1950). The store, the Grand Opera House above, and my grandparent's home were connected buildings known as the The Steinberg Block. The location was on Front Street, still the center of the business district in Traverse City. At the back flowed the Boardman River, but logs no longer floated on it. The lumbering business had long since declined.

When grandfather Julius was asked to run for mayor of Traverse City, he is said to have declined with the explanation that "A politician has both friends and enemies, a businessman can afford to have only friends."

Grandfather Julius was an energetic man, short and of sturdy build. Even in later life when I knew him, he was full of energy and interest in what was going on in the world. He was interested in government and politics, and was ready to enjoy a political argument at the drop of a hat. From my earliest recollection we enjoyed arguments on politics in our family. As I look back, this kind of fun was introduced by my grandfather Julius. He was a Republican, and he reflected the early settler's philosophy of rugged individualism. By the time his grandchildren came along times had changed, the West was settled, and Woodrow Wilson was striving to replace rugged individualism with ways for people to get along together in a more crowded society. We had many an exciting argument about minimum wages and about local option (whether the county should be wet or dry). My father and grandfather taking the businessman's view and my brother and I the moral issue.

Grandfather Julius lived to the age of seventy-six. He died in Detroit in 1923 following a short illness.

CHICKEN SOUP

3-4 lb. chicken	1 Tbl. salt
3 carrots	2 stalks celery with tops
3 parsnips	¼ tsp. pepper
1 large onion, studded with 3 whole cloves	1 bay leaf

Wash chicken, cut up or leave whole. Cover with water in a 6 qt. pot and bring to a boil. While boiling, keep skimming foam from top until none remains (about 5-10 minutes). More water may have to be added at this point to keep the chicken covered. Add remaining ingredients and cook gently for 1½ hours, with cover tilted. Discard vegetables, remove chicken and chill broth. When soup is cold, any fat can easily be skimmed from top. Serve hot with matzo balls if desire.

*   *   *

MATZO BALLS
(Knaidlach)

4 eggs, separated	4 qts. boiling water
1 c. matzo meal	¾ tsp. salt

Beat egg whites till stiff. Beat egg yolks. Fold whites into yolks, then fold in matzo meal and salt. Refrigerate for 1 hour. Wet hands with water, divide into 12 pieces and make into balls. Drop into water and cook for 20 minutes. Remove with slotted spoon.

*   *   *

By Erni Goldstein

BRAIDED EGG BREAD
(Challah)

¼ c. warm water	1 Tbl. yeast
1 Tbl. sugar	

Stir yeast and sugar into water in small bowl - let sit till foamy, about 5-10 minutes.

1 Tbl. sugar	½ c. warm water
1 tsp. salt	2¾ c. flour (approx.)
1 egg	1 tsp. sesame seeds
1 Tbl. oil	

Mix together. Add yeast mixture and stir well with wooden spoon till dough is smooth. Add more flour, if necessary to handle well. Turn onto floured board and knead for 10 minutes. Place in greased bowl and turn so that dough is well greased. Cover with a cloth and let rise in warm place for 1 hour. Punch down, cover and let rise for ½ hour. Divide dough into 3 equal parts and roll into 14 inch strands with lightly greased hands. Braid on a greased baking sheet, pinch ends together. Brush with oil, cover with a towel and let rise for 45 minutes. Brush egg mixture on top and sides of bread, sprinkle with sesame seeds. Bake at 350 degrees for 30 minutes.

Egg mixture: 1 egg   1 tsp. honey   1 Tbl. water

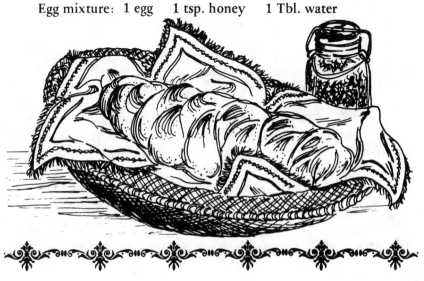

STUFFED CABBAGE
(Holishkes)

2 small cans tomato paste
1 small can water
½ c. raisins
4 Tbl. brown sugar
¾ c. honey

Juice of 1 lemon
½ c. graham cracker
  crumbs
Salt to taste

Stir together all ingredients. Add cabbage rolls and cook over medium heat for about 1½ hours till meat is cooked. Serve over rice.

2 lbs. chopped chuck
1 medium onion, grated
1 c. matzo meal or bread
  crumbs

1 tsp salt
1 egg

Mix together well. Put 1 heaping tablespoonful in center of leaf and roll up. Place in sauce seam side down. Any leftover stuffing can be baked as meatloaf.

1 large head cabbage
Separate leaves, steam 8-10 minutes, till soft.

*　　　　*　　　　*

CHOPPED LIVER

½ c. oil or chicken fat
2 medium onions, sliced
1 lb. chicken livers

4 eggs, hard boiled
1½ tsp. salt
¼ tsp. pepper

Melt ¼ c. fat in skillet and saute onions for about 10 minutes. Remove onions and set aside. Melt remaining fat in same skillet and saute liver for 10 minutes, till brown. Stir occasionally. Chop onions, liver and eggs in wooden bowl or food processor till fine.

Serve cold on crackers or on a sandwich with lettuce.

*　　　　*　　　　*

VEGETARIAN CHOPPED LIVER

1 lb. can string beans,
   well drained
4 hard boiled eggs

2 Tbl. oil
2 medium chopped onions
Salt and pepper to taste

Saute onions in oil till brown, drain off oil. In wooden bowl or food processor add onions, eggs and string beans, chop till fine. Add salt and pepper if desired. Serve cold on crackers or on a sandwich with lettuce.

       *   *   *

CHEESE BLINTZES

1 c. flour
1 c. water
3 eggs

½ tsp. salt
1 Tbl. butter

Mix well till smooth. Using a heated and greased 6 inch frying pan, pour about ¼ c. batter in pan, tilt pan quickly so that entire bottom of pan is covered. Quickly pour off any extra batter. Cook till pancake is lightly brown on bottom. Remove from pan, onto counter with brown side facing up. Repeat till all batter is used.

¼ lb. ricotta
¼ lb. cream cheese
   softened
¼ lb. cottage cheese

1 egg
2 Tbl. matzo meal
3 Tbl. sugar
1 tsp. vanilla

Mix together. Fill each pancake with about 1 Tbl. filling on brown side. Fold sides into center, overlapping so filling won't spill out. Can be frozen or cooked at this point. To freeze, place seam side down in freezer container. To bake, melt ½ c. butter or margarine in 9x13 inch pan. Place blintzes seam side down in hot pan and bake at 375 degrees for 30-45 minutes, till brown.

Serve with sour cream or applesauce.

POTATO PANCAKES
(Potato Latkes)

6 medium potatoes,
  unpared
1 medium onion, grated
2 eggs

Oil for frying
3 Tbl. flour or matzo meal
½ tsp. baking powder
1 tsp. salt

Grate raw potatoes and drain well. Grate onion and add to potatoes with eggs and salt. Mix well. Combine flour and baking powder and add to above mixture, mixing well. Drop by spoonfuls into hot oil, brown well on both sides, drain on paper towel. Serve hot with applesauce or sour cream.

*   *   *

NOODLE PUDDING
(Lukshen Kugel)

1 lb. broad noodles
6 eggs
¼ lb. butter, melted
1 lb. 4 oz. can crushed
  pineapple

1 c. sugar
6 oz. can frozen orange
  juice
3 Tbl. lemon juice

Cook noodles for about 5 minutes, drain well. Beat eggs and add with rest of ingredients to noodles. Pour into 9x13 greased pan and bake at 350 degrees for 1 hour.

*   *   *

Wooden Shoes on the Golf Course

If you see an eighty-one-year-old man on the golf course shooting in the lows 70s while wearing wooden shoes, you can be sure it's Fred Oldemulders -- the nation's oldest wooden shoemaker.

"I can play as good a game in wooden shoes as I can in golf shoes," said Oldemulders, a resident of Holland on Michigan's west coast. "If you want to play a game of golf of eighteen holes, I take a pair of wooden shoes and walk along with you just as good as you do in other shoes."

Oldemulders came to the United States in 1923, mirgrating with his new wife from the small village of Laars on the Netherlands-Germany border. He left the old country because it was almost financially impossible to begin a home and household in Europe at that time. Mrs. Oldemulders had relatives who would sponsor the couple in Holland and, so, the couple set up housekeeping in Michigan.

During his early years in the Netherlands, Oldemulders followed the criteria of the village where the boys were taught the trade of their fathers. Oldemulders followed in the footsteps of his brothers and began making shoes at the age of fifteen. He said it took him three winters to master the trade. Winters because the summers were spent working on the farm.

Following his migration to America, Oldemulders opened a small wooden shoe shop in his home. In 1925 he went to work in a local funiture factory while working nights on the shoes to add to his income.

The craftsman found an outlet for his shoes with the Dutch Novelty Shop, owned and operated by the late Chester and Mae Van Tongeren. The name of the plant was changed fifty years ago to the Wooden Shoe Factory and is still operated by members of the Van Tongeren family. With the changing of the name, old world shoemak-

By William H. Vande Water

17

Fred Oldemulders at Work

ing machines were added. Oldemulders made shoes by hand and machine from that time on. Today modern machines are along side the more than one-hundred-year-old machines which are still operating.

With the beginning of the Tulip Time Festival in Holland in 1929, the demand for wooden shoes increased. Oldemulders alone carved all the shoes for the Klompen Dancers (wooden shoe teams) the first few years of the festival.

Today with dancers numbering nearly one thousand for each festival, Oldemulders and his craftsmen work long hours producing good fitting shoes for the dancers.

Between 1939 -- when he purchased a European wooden shoe machine to augment his hand production -- and 1964, he turned out 300,000 pairs of wooden shoes.

"The highest number of shoes in one year that I made with two other men helping me was 18,000 pair," Oldemulders said.

When making wooden shoes, Oldemulders quarters the various pieces of logs. A size eight shoe requires a log section twelve inches long. The aspen logs come from trees grown on sandy soil in Michigan and Indiana. Sandy soil produces wood without a "wet" or dark center. Most of the trees are grown on high ground.

He does the initial shaping with a wide-bladed hand axe or hatchet. He then moves to the six-foot long bench. It is made of an aspen log with the top quarter sawed for a flat side. Attached to this side is a long block knife -- one he brought from the old country. The big knife gives him great leverage and the shoe takes shape after only a couple of dozen turns under the blade.

The shoes are then placed in a block vise, which is also part of the log bench. It is a square eight-inch area cut out of the side of the log. The two shoes are placed in the slot, held in place by a wedge of of wood. Oldemulders uses a T-shaped "spoon chisel" to hollow out the inside of the shoe. It is this step that separates the woodworker from the shoemakers, Oldemulder, says.

"I tailor each pair of shoes for each customer," he said. "We have feet with high insteps, low insteps, flat feet, all kinds of feet."

Oldemulders makes all the patterns, or "mols," for the various sizes and types of shoes made in the Wooden Shoe Factory.

The shoes are finished and smoothed off by a sharp home-made knife made from a file. The shoes are then sanded smoothly on the outside and are ready for wear.

Many dignitaries in goverment and figures in sports, arts and the media own shoes made by Oldemulders. To name a few: former Presidents Dwight Eisenhower, John Kennedy, Richard Nixon and Gerald Ford; Governors Kim Sigler, G. Mennen Williams, George Romney and William G. Milliken; TV starsBob Hope, Arlene Francis, Arthur Godfrey; sports figures Al Kaline, Dave Rozema, Mark "The

Bird" Fidrych, Bo Schembeckler and Walter Hagen. Many heads of royalty and government on their visit to Michigan's Holland have received a pair of wooden shoes with their names engraved on them, as a symbol of the city.

Although Dutch-Americans wear as many as six pairs of socks with wooden shoes, Oldemulders said in the old country only one pair was worn at a time.

"In the summer time when we were finished with our farm work, or if it was raining so we could not do farm work, we were given enough yarn - mostly hand spun - to make a pair of socks." he said. "We had learned to knit early in life, so we each made at least two pairs of socks. We had wooden shoes for outdoor work, for church and for special occasions. If we were fortunate, we had a pair of leather shoes."

He also said only one pair of socks is needed if you get a good wooden shoe fit.

Oldemulders wears out about two pairs of wooden shoes each year. Although he'll defend them for comfort any day against other shoes, he's not permitted to wear them in two of his favorite places.

"I can't wear them in the kitchen, dining room or sitting room in my house, although a sneak-in is permissible," he said

The second place is the bowling alley where "no other shoes are permissible but bowling shoes."

PIGS IN THE BLANKET
(Saucijzebroodjes)

2½ c. white flour	½ c. milk or more
2 tsp. baking powder	1 lb. of pork steak and
2 tsp. salt	1 lb. of veal steak,
½ c. lard	ground together
1 egg	Salt and pepper

Mix and sift ingredients. Cut in the shortening as for pie crust. Beat the egg and add milk to dry ingredients. More milk may be needed to make a soft dough of proper consistency to roll out into about ¼ inch thickness. Season the meat and make into small rolls about 4 inches long and ½ inch in thickness. Wrap each roll with the pastry, pinching ends. Bake in hot oven 20-30 minutes, in bake pans, until brown.

*   *   *

FAVORED DUTCH DISH
(Balkenbrij)

1½ lb. liver	2 lb. of pork
1 lb. of beef	Buckwheat flour

Cook liver well done. Cook beef and save the juice. Chop both. Season well, with salt, pepper, sage, celery salt and spices if desired. Add pork to meat broth. Bring to a boil and stir in buckwheat flour until stiff. Meat is chopped before putting in kettle. Cook for 1 hour after adding flour. Put in buttered pans.

After cooling cut in slices and fry.

*   *   *

By William H. Vande Water

ALMOND COOKIES
(Amandel Kokenes)

6 egg yolks   1 c. flour
1½ c. sugar   1 tsp. baking powder
½ lb. fine ground almond

Beat egg yolks, add sugar and almonds and blend well. Add flour sifted with baking powder.

Roll out on lightly floured board and cut with a cookie cutter into desired shapes. Place on greased cookie sheet. Bake in a 325 degree oven 12-15 minutes.

*   *   *

RAW POTATO PATTIES
(Rauw Aardappel Past Ertje)

6 large potatoes, grated 1 Tbl. flour
1 medium sized onion 1 tsp. salt
3 eggs well beaten

Drain potatoes well in sieve by pressing out water. Put into mixing bowl and add other ingredients. Stir until well mixed.

Drop by tablespoons into hot fat, or make patties and fry slowly until golden brown on both sides. Serve with applesauce.

*   *   *

CUT GREEN BEAN SALAD
(Snijboontjes Salade)

Shred equal parts of cabbage, carrots and green beans. Add onion and green pepper to suit taste. Mix with any desired salad dressing. Serve on crisp lettuce leaf, and sprinkle top with very thinly sliced green beans.

*   *   *

JAN HOCGEL COOKIES

1 c. sugar
1 c. butter or margarine
2 c. flour

½ tsp. cinnamon
1 egg yolk
½ c. finely chopped nuts
1 egg white

Mix the first five ingredients real good with wooden spoon. Spread on cookie sheet. Spread ½ c. finely chopped nuts, thin. Mix the egg white well with small tsp. of water and spread on top of the nuts.

Bake at 350 degrees for 15 minutes or so depending on the oven. Cut warm in the size you want them.

*   *   *

FAT BALLS
(Vet Bollen)

2 c. flour
1 c. milk
1½ c. sugar
2 eggs

1 tsp. salt
1 c. raisins
3 tsp. baking powder

Mix in order given, and drop from spoon into hot deep fat. Fry about 3 minutes.

*   *   *

HODGE PODGE
(Hutspot)

Boil separately until tender; 6 carrots, 6 onions, 8 potatoes. Drain well and mix together. Add salt and pepper to taste. Add a good size piece of butter, and stew together with sweet milk.

*   *   *

ALMOND ROLLS
(Banket)

1 c. sugar
1 egg
1 c. of almond or
  macaroon paste
1 egg, separated

¼ c. of cornstarch
2 c. flour
1 c. butter
¼ c. water

Put sugar, egg, paste, egg yolk and cornstarch in a bowl and let stand for ½ hour. Blend flour, butter and water in a bowl. Preheat oven to 400 degrees. Divide dough into two parts. Roll dough on floured board. Cut lengthwise into equal strips (4 strips, each is 4x 13 inches in all).

Place the filling on length of dough. Fold over the short ends. Follow with folding the long sides, moistening with water on one side to seal before pressing. Place with seam side down on a cookie sheet, make small holes on top for air. Beat egg white and brush the top of the rolls.

Bake 15 minutes at 400 degrees and then at 325 degrees for 20 minutes or until light brown.

*   *   *

BUTTER COOKIES IN THE SHAPE OF A FIGURE 8
(Krakelingen)

2 c. butter
4 c. flour

½ c. water
sugar

Cut butter into flour and stir in water gradually, making a dough similar to a pastry. Cover and refrigerate over night. Preheat oven to 375 degrees. Roll small amount of dough into pencil shape, bring ends together and twist like a figure 8. Dip both sides into sugar; place on an ungreased cookie sheet. Bake until brown on bottom. Makes 6 dozen.

DUTCH PEPPER CAKE
(Hollandsche Peper Koek)

1 c. brown sugar	2 c. flour
½ c. shortening	½ c. cold water
2 eggs	1 tsp. ginger
1 tsp. soda	1 tsp. cinnamon
½ c. molasses	

Cream sugar and shortening. Add eggs which have been beaten. Stir soda into molassess, add to mixture. Next add water. Sift spices and pinch of salt with flour. Add to mixture. Bake in a slow oven (about 325 degrees) about 40 minutes.

*   *   *

DUTCH HARD CANDY
(Hollandsche Babelaars)

1 c. brown sugar	½ c. vinegar
1 c. white sugar	1/3 c. water
Butter - size of a walnut	

Mix ingredients. Bring to a boil and continue boiling without stirring until a spoonful dropped into cold water becomes crisp. Pour into buttered pans and as soon as cool enough to handle, butter hands and pull into long strips. Cut at once with buttered scissors to size of pieces wanted.

*   *   *

EGG NOG I

3 well beaten eggs	1 pt. milk
3 tsp. sugar	½ c. brandy

Mix eggs, sugar, and milk. Add brandy while stirring.

EGG NOG II
(Advocaat)

Beat egg yolks until very thick and mix with equal amount of brandy. Add sugar to taste and finish with a dash of nutmeg.

Two would-be Klompen Dancers are ready to celebrate Holland's Tulip Festival. *(Photo from Michigan State Photo Archives)*

The Golden Streets of Delray

When I was a boy, I asked my parents why they came to America.

My mother, who was born in Germany but later moved to Hungary as a child, came because her parents died at an early age, leaving three children homeless. Relatives decided to farm them out to aunts and uncles with financial means to care for them. And so, my mother came to America at sixteen, to live with an aunt in Delray in 1906.

My father had a more adventurous answer.

"I heard often that the streets of America were paved in gold and that it was a cornucopia, a land of plenty," he said.

He also told me his dreams were soon shattered. While on the train from New York to Detroit each immigrant was handed a big box of chocolate candy. After about thirty minutes the conductor came down the aisle collecting two dollars for each box. I asked him what he did. He said, "Even though I ate six or seven pieces, I put the lid back on and returned the candy."

My father settled on the west side of Detroit, in Delray, on the same block as my mother. Both being lonesome and lost in this vast, new land, they soon married and raised a family of six children, three boys and three girls. I was born number four in line on Valentine's Day, 1919. This was the year of the great influenza epidemic in the United States. I was told by my parents that more babies died than survived during that epidemic. My brothers and sisters, in order of birth, are Kalman, Mathilda, Edward, Rosemary and Martha.

My education began in the first grade at Morley School in Delray. It was located on Pulaski Avenue in a heavily populated Polish neighborhood. St. John Cansius Church and elementary school was just down the block. It's enrollment was one hundred percent Polish. In just the opposite direction was located Holy Cross Church and school, with its enrollment one hundred percent Hungarian.

I attended Morley School until the end of my fourth grade. Like my brothers and sisters before me, I was transferred to Holy

By Arthur Bator

Cross where we were prepared for our First Holy Communion and Confirmation. This took about two years.

After these two years I became very disenchanted with Holy Cross. The parish priest and the nuns insisted I pronounce my name Bah-tor, instead of Bay-tor and they constantly reminded me that Bahtor was a beautiful Hungarian name, meaning "brave".

I didn't care how beautifully Hungarian it was; I felt I was an American kid. My brothers were in high school and they were known as Kal and Eddie Baytor, football, baseball, basketball, and track stars, so I wanted to be known as Art Baytor and dreamed of following in their footsteps.

But I must give credit to those little nuns. Whether it was taught in English or in Hungarian, they pounded it into my head, and, ah, how they pounded, on and on. I will now admit that it was one of the reasons I wanted to leave and go to Morley School again.

We were expected to go to Confession in Hungarian and I found it difficult to confess English sins in Hungarian. This was one of my excuses in begging to return to Morley School. My father would have been happy and proud to have his son's name pronounced Bahtor and continue with his Hungarian traditions but my mother, being basically German and a transplanted, converted Hungarian, understood my problem, so back to Morley School I went where I finished my elementary education.

It was during these grade school days, about fourth grade, that I remember a "slight" introduction to sex. Sex was an unknown word in our family. Everything that was born was delivered by the stork.

One day a neighbor boy and I became involved in a ferocious fight. I bloodied up his face and fractured his nose. To top it off, I was stuffing horse manure (left by the milk wagon horses) into his mouth when his father ran out of the house, grabbed me around the neck, and marched me into my father's drug store. My father listened to this man and saw the bloody evidence standing next to him. Without asking too many questions my father shook me up and sent me upstairs to wait. Then my father explained the situation to my mother and went back downstairs to attend his business.

Mother, being less excitable, quietly asked me why I did it, because this wasn't like me. Finally I told her that he called her "Fatty Arbuckle". Fatty Arbuckle in our day was a very fat movie comedian.

Immediately my mother understood; a slow smile came over her face as she gently stroked my head and even gave me a popsicle before I went back out to play.

Two days later my kid sister, Martha, was born – delivered by the stork, naturally.

When I entered high school we moved out of the Delray area, but remained on the west side of Detroit, where I attended Southwestern High School with the same kids I had gone to school with at Morley, Holy Cross and St. John Cansius. Also it was the same high school my brothers and sisters attended. It was a real melting pot of Detroit, with everybody having a different ethnic background.

My new neighborhood was made up of Canadian, English, and second and third generation Americans. I soon learned that they all had mothers and fathers, not "mudders" and "fadders". They said "this", not "dis", and "that", not "dat".

Six months after leaving Delray, I went back there to visit the kids I had hung around with and every one told me I talked funny. I knew what they meant: as I was leaving, I said, "I'll be seeing you fellas," instead of the customary, "I'll be seeing youse guys." I was really beginning to feel American.

What I noticed at Southwestern High was the fact the kids who participated in athletics went at it harder if they came from an ethnic family.

When we played football against schools like Cooley High and Mackenzie High we tried harder and usually ended up on top. They were new beautiful high schools in the then suburban area of Detroit. It was where the high salaried, fifty-dollar-a-week executives moved their families. These newer schools always had their hands full with Southwestern; and Southwestern always had their hands full with Hamtramck High, which was 115 per cent Polish, and tough!

Incidentally, in the process of knocking heads, we did get an education and finished school. My brothers and I attended Michigan, Michigan State, and Detroit City College (now Wayne State). The war continued at home; who was better -- Michigan or Michigan State.

The traditions I remember most vividly pertain mostly to language, food and our Christmas.

At home, my parents always spoke their native language, as did all of us children. When we reached high school, we spoke English and Hungarian simultaneously. I can never remember knowing the two languages individually. We also spoke a third language, which for lack of a better word, I'll call "Gibberish." When we could not express ourselves to our parents in English or Hungarian, we came up with a combination of the two.

As the years went on we pretty much spoke English to each other. I never learned to read or write in the Hungarian language but until about fifteen years ago, before my parents died, I was complimented many times on how well I spoke the language. Today I understand the language perfectly, but I grope for words, when speaking it.

I will always feel that nobody ever lived who could cook as well as my mother. Without a recipe and with her wooden stirring spoon, she could concoct heavenly meals. I always felt we were specially blessed children to be the ones chosen to eat my mother's cooking.

When I asked her to teach my wife how to cook "our" dishes, her answer was always "a pinch of this and a dash of that." Even though my wife became a fine cook, when it came to American dishes, I honestly could never give her more than a "C" as a Hungarian cook.

I could list and describe my mother's special dishes, page after page, but it would only break my heart to remember what I no longer can taste or have. To truly appreciate what I'm talking about the reader would have had to taste the food.

Chrismas to us kids at home was a fantasy land. It all started on the fifth of December, when we polished our shoes, made cornucopia type cones out of newspaper, inserted them inside our shoes, along with our list to Santa Claus. Early morning of the following day, Saint Nicholas day, we would run to the window and find the note gone, but the shoes filled to the brim with nuts, candy, dates, and figs.

From that moment on until Christmas we would be under the wonderful spell. During this time we would find tinsel, mysteriously dropped in various parts of the house, clusters of Christmas candy behind curtains and strange foot prints in the snow outside our windows.

All this time we were as good and saintly as the elves and angels who were doing these wonderful deeds for us. As we grew older and knew it was Mom who was behind this, we would not let on because we didn't want to spoil it for her OR for ourselves. So we "believed" longer than we dared admit, even to this day.

All the while this was going on the house was being cleaned and prepared for Christmas. Because of the lack of refrigeration the baking was left until December twenty-third. We didn't dare run through the house because next to every radiator a pan of dough was rising.

This was also the night we spread a large sheet on the floor where Santa and his helpers would place a huge tree. Nobody saw the tree until after dinner on Christmas Eve, when suddenly a tiny bell would ring, the door would open -- and there in front of us was our fantasy world.

Another tradition we observed was the melting of lead as part of our New Year's Eve celebration. Each of us would melt a few ounces of lead in a tablespoon over the gas stove. When the lead became molten we poured it into a large glass of cold water. When we retrieved it in its strange form, we tried to imagine what it indicated. From this we would then tell our fortune for the coming year.

When I arrived in East Lansing in 1953, I was employed by a local ophthalmologist, Dr. Arthur E. Schultz. After many chats at work and on hunting trips, we were surprised that our backgrounds were very similar.

While working his way through medical school, he was a projectionist at a Delray movie theater. Even today we exchange many memories of the various Hungarian foods and customs, and we take great pleasure trying to stump each other with difficult Hungarian words.

Now, as I look back through my life as a businessman, I feel that I have been moderately successful and I give thanks to two people; Dr. Schultz, who showed me how to make money, and my mother, who taught me how to save and spend it properly.

I'm grateful for my ethnic background because it has helped me to better understand the problems of minority races and to pass this understanding on to my children. Most of all, I thank God that my parents met in America and raised me an American, where, indeed, "the streets are paved in gold."

CHICKEN PAPRIKASH

2 chopped onions	2 Tbl. salt
4 Tbl. shortening	5 lb. chicken in pieces
2 Tbl. paprika	1 c. water
1 tsp. black pepper	1 c. sour cream

Saute onion in shortening; add seasonings and chicken; saute about 10 minutes. Add water. Cover and simmer until chicken is tender. Remove chicken. Add sour cream to pan drippings and mix well. Serve with dumplings or noodles. Serves four.

*   *   *

HUNGARIAN SCALLOPED POTATOES WITH SAUSAGE

8 medium potatoes, boiled in skins	¼ lb. butter or margarine, melted
8 hard-boiled eggs	1 c. bread crumbs
¾ lb. smoked sausage, thinley sliced	1 c. sour cream
	1 tsp. salt

Place 3 tsp. melted butter in bottom of casserole. Add 3 tsp. crumbs, sprinkled over butter. Put layer of sliced potatoes, a layer of sausage and a layer of sliced hard-cooked egg. Add salt. Sprinkle 4 tsp. melted butter and 4 tsp. bread crumbs over egg layer. Continue in this manner until all ingredients are in casserole. Pour sour cream on top and bake at 350 degrees about 1 hour or until golden brown.

*   *   *

By Suzanne Gyeszly

DUMPLINGS

3 beaten eggs	½ Tbl. salt
2 c. flour	1/3 c. water
2 Tbl. oil	

Mix all ingredients together and beat with spoon. Drop batter by teaspoonful into boiling salted water. Cook about 10 minutes. Drain and rinse with cold water. Add to paprikash.

*   *   *

DRUM TORTE
(Dobos Torta)

10 egg yolks	10 egg whites
9 Tbl. sugar	¼ tsp. salt
1 Tbl. baking powder	Grated rind of 1 lemon
10 level Tbl. flour	

Beat egg yolks for 5 minutes and add sugar, by spoonfuls, until lemon colored and fluffy. Sift flour, baking powder and salt and mix with egg yolk mixture until smooth (about 5 minutes), and add grated rind of whole lemon. Lightly fold in beaten egg whites. Grease and flour 9 inch cake pans and spoon in thin layer of mix. Bake in 350 degree oven for 10 minutes. Makes 6-7 layers.

Icing for Dobos Torta:

¾ lb. unsalted butter	1 tsp. vanilla
1 c. confectionary sugar	½ c. cocoa
1 whole egg	1/3 c. black coffee, cold

Cream butter and sugar. Beat in egg. Add cocoa, vanilla and beat until smooth. Add coffee. Spread small amount of icing on each layer and stack them and ice outside and top of cake also.

*   *   *

SOUR CHERRY SOUP

1 can sour cherries or	Salt
fresh sour cherries	Sugar
1 qt. water	1 inch cinnamon stick
1 pt. sour cream	1 Tbl. flour

Bring water and cherries to boil and add cinnamon, salt. Blend thoroughly the flour in the sour cream and gradually add to soup and simmer for 10 minutes and add sugar to taste.

*   *   *

HUNGARIAN GOULASH SOUP

1 lb. beef flank	2 stalks celery
2 Tbl. lard	1 fresh tomato
2 large onions	4 medium size potatoes
1 green pepper	½ tsp. paprika
2 large carrots	1 tsp. salt
2 parsley roots and	1/8 tsp. black pepper
greens	2 qt. water

Cut meat into squares, wash. Saute onion in lard, add paprika, stir well, add meat, salt, and ¼ c. of water. Cook slowly for 1 hour. Add all of washed and diced vegetables but potatoes. Add another cup of water and cook slowly for ½ hour. Add potatoes, continue cooking for 15 minutes. Add 1 qt. of cold water, let it come to a boil and cook for 10 minutes. Serve as a main dish.

*   *   *

HUNGARIAN NUT OR POPPYSEED ROLLS

2 heaping Tbl. sugar	1 Tbl. sugar
½ lb. butter	5 c. all-purpose flour
4 egg yolks	Pinch of salt
1 pkg. yeast	Grated rind of a lemon or orange
½ c. lukewarm water	

Cream butter with 2 Tbl. sugar and add egg yolks. Dissolve yeast in lukewarm water with 1 Tbl. sugar and add sifted flour with salt and with grated lemon rind. Mix well and knead on a floured board (if dough seems a little stiff add ¼ to ½ c. sour cream to make a more pliable dough). Divide dough into 3 parts; let rest, covered in a large bowl for at least an hour. Roll each piece into a rectangle. Fill with nuts or poppyseed and place into a greased baking pan. Let rise again for 30-40 minutes. Brush tops with beaten egg and bake in moderate oven at 350 degrees for 30 minutes.

Nut filling:
> 1 lb. walnuts, ground fine 1 Tbl. vanilla
> 1 c. sugar

Melt the sugar, then add the nuts and cook with a little milk to the desired consistency. Add the vanilla and allow to cool before spreading.

*   *   *

By Judy Gyurko

CHICKEN GIBLETS AND RICE

½ c. onions, chopped
¼ c. shortening
1 tsp. paprika
1 c. raw long grain rice

2 c. water
Salt and pepper
1 lb. chicken giblets

Saute onion in hot shortening until soft, add paprika and giblets. Stir to coat, cover and cook over a low flame 20 minutes. Then add water and seasonings, continue to simmer until almost done. Check broth, there should be about 2 c. Replace with additional water if liquid is cooked down too much. Now add washed rice and stir gently. Cover and continue to simmer until rice is tender. Cook on as low a flame as possible so liquid does not evaporate. Garnish with chopped parsley.

*   *   *

WALNUT PITA

2 c. all-purpose
   flour
2 Tbl. sugar
Pinch of salt

½ lb. butter
1 egg yolk
¼ pt. sour cream

Mix all ingredients as for pie dough, divide into 2 pieces. Roll each piece large enough to line a 9x12 pan. Line bottom of pan with one rolled dough, add filling and place other piece of dough on top and bake for 30-40 minutes at 350 degrees or until golden brown.

Filling:

6 egg yolks
1 c. sugar

½ lb. ground walnuts
7 egg whites stiffly beaten

Beat together egg yolks and sugar, add walnuts, fold in egg white that has been stiffly beaten.

Sprinkle with powdered sugar before serving.

DOUBLE DECKER PASTRY
(Linzer Slices)

5 c. sifted all-purpose flour	4 egg yolks beaten slightly
4 tsp. baking powder	½ pt. sour cream
2 tsp. baking soda	1 tsp. vanilla
¼ tsp. salt	2½ c. ground nuts (English walnuts)
1 c. sugar	½ c. sugar
½ lb. sweet butter	Apricot jam or lekvar (plum butter)
2 Tbl. shortening	

Sift dry ingredients, add sugar, cut in shortenings as for pie crust. Add egg yolks, sour cream and vanilla, mix well, divide dough into 3 parts. Roll out first piece on floured board to thickness of pie crust. Place in ungreased 10x15 inch pan letting dough come up about 1/3 of the way around the sides. Combine nuts and ½ c. sugar and spread all but a handful over dough. Place over nut mixture second piece of rolled dough and spread with apricot (or other) jam or lekvar. Sprinkle reserved sugar nut mixture over jam, roll out third piece of dough, cut in strips and criss cross on top.

Bake in 350 degree oven 25-30 minutes or until done. Cut in squares or diamond shapes and sprinkle a little powered sugar on top before serving.

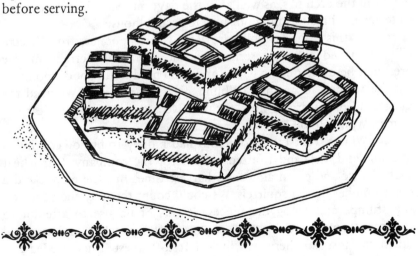

Little Wheat;
A Lot of Mosquitoes

The following passage is from "Pioneer Life in the Big Dane Settlement," written by August Rasmussen. Mr. Rasmussen, who lived in Montcalm County, left Denmark in 1856 when he was twenty-seven on a long and stormy voyage with his bride to live forty-six years in the Big Dane Settlement.

If ever there was a busy people, it was we Dane folks. We cleared land, and put in some wheat. We cut down trees, hewed them on two sides, and put up a nice schoolhouse well shingled. We elected a schoolboard, and hired a Miss Haskell for a teacher. But, alas! Miss Haskell could not understand the children, and the children could not understand Miss Haskell. The children went to school wearing wooden shoes; and, oh! what a noise they made.

Bicycles and golden nose-glasses were not in style then in those days. Roads were too new for that. The times called for business, and study, and learning; and the children learned fast, too. The teacher learned to speak Danish, and the children learned to speak English, and the parents, too. Miss Haskell was a good teacher. She taught in the evenings, as well as in the daytime. She did all she could to teach and break us in in our new log schoolhouse.

In this same schoolhouse Rev. Chas. Spooner, from Greenville, preached the first sermon in the Big Dane Settlement. He preached here for quite a while, and tried hard to do good among us, and he warned us against a "blind pig" in Greenville. We need the same kind of a warning now, for we have a "blind pig" now near our homes. Who will kill it?

Winter went by. Those who had money to live on continued clearing land; C.J. and I rafted lumber for the company. Our wheat looked nice and green almost to harvest time. But there appeared a great number of red squirrels. We could count them by the dozen on the stumps and along the fences. It was of no use to attempt to frighten them. They bit off one head after another, and tramped down the rest, so there was little left to harvest. I had seeded five bushels of good wheat, and harvested but five and one-half bushels! This was a sad disappointment.

A great affliction followed. Our bright and beautiful boy was suddenly taken sick. Dr. Slawson was not to be had. We used remedies as best we knew to relieve his pain, but all in vain. He died February 20, 1859, at 7 o'clock P.M. This, our child, was the first born, and the first buried in the Big Dane Settlement. We dug his grave among the bushes, logs, and standing trees, where now is our beautiful graveyard, where men and women and children have been laid to rest ever since.

Hard times came. There was no steady work at the sawmill. My shoes were worn out. So I said to my wife, I must go to work a few weeks to earn something to eat. I got me a pair of wooden shoes made by a neighbor, put them on and started on the same way I came in, by Wolverton Plains. Coming to the four corners where the little church stands, I found Mr. Wise plowing. He stopped his team and asked where I was going. I told him I was looking for a job. As he rested his arms on the fence he noticed my wooden shoes, and said, "Those would be good for killing some of the many squirrels we have this year." "Yes, indeed." said I, "if you catch them I can kill them." And we both laughed. "Do you know who has a little job of work?" I inquired. He answered, "Well, if you will thrash with a flail, you may work at both my crops, wheat and oats. You can have every tenth bushel for your work and I furnish the machine."

Danes Harvesting near Greenville (*Photo from Michigan State Photo Archives*)

39

I took the job and began work right off. The machine furnished by Mr. Wise was two sticks of wood tied together with a buckskin strap, one stick or pole longer than the other. With this machine I commenced flailing on his barn floor and finished his job, and afterwards, also, one for Mr. Fuller. I earned in all fifteen bushels of wheat and forty bushels of oats. It was early in September and hard work in the hot days. It took me near a month. At this time my brother and I had an ox team and I drew home all the grain I had earned in two loads.

When I went home after the first week's work, Mr. Wise said that if my wife would pick him a bushel of blackberries he would give her a bushel of wheat, and if I would seed down ten acres of wheat ground, he would give me another bushel of wheat. We made a bargain and I went home and told my wife.

The next Monday I returned to my job and my wife commenced picking blackberries. Twenty rods south east of our house is a hollow in which those days was a great windfall where blackberries were abundant, and here she began to pick berries. She had one pail full and began another when she heard a noise nearby, and along came a black bear walking the trunk of a big pine tree. Through fear she made a great outcry and fell over the trunk of another tree. Frightened by all the noise, the bear took his way east into the woods and my wife finished picking her bushel of berries. In those days bears were around here. One morning Mr. Whenwood killed three down next to the creek, right west of here.

Well, Mr. Wise received the berries, and I was paid the wheat. He at the time was well off, and I was poor, but we were a mutual help to each other, and that is what people should ever strive to be.

That year we had little wheat and a superabundance of squirrels and mosquitoes. In pioneer days, generally, noses are kept somewhat near the ground.

Summer had gone, and six bushels of wheat had been sown. My wife placed over the grave of our son the first flower plant in our graveyard–a rose bush.

ROAST GOOSE FOR CHRISTMAS
(Stegt Julegaas)

10-12 lb. goose	6 Tbl. butter
Salt	2 lb. tart apples
Flour	1 lb. prunes

Select a young goose. Singe, wash carefully with hot water, both inside and out, then salt both inside and out. Stuff with apples which have been pared, cored and quartered, and then mixed with prunes which have been soaked, pitted and cut in halves. Put in very hot oven (450 degrees) for 45 minutes. Then remove and drain all fat from pan. Sprinkle goose all over with salt and dredge with flour. Return to oven, lower the temperature to 350 degrees and keep it there. Allow in all, 20 minutes roasting per pound. When flour has browned, start basting with hot water in which butter has been melted. Baste frequently. Sprinkle lightly with flour after each basting. This is a popular holiday dish. With it are served red cabbage and browned potatoes.

*   *   *

MARINATED HERRING
(Spegesildi Marinade)

Sauce:

¼ c. sour cream	3 Tbl. vinegar
2 Tbl. sugar	1 slice onion

Remove skin and bones from 2 salted herring. Cut in bite size pieces. Then soak in cold water 1 hour. Drain. Arrange the herring in a low bowl and cover with the sauce.

*   *   *

DANISH PASTRY
(Dansk Wienerbrod)

¼ c. warm milk	1 c. coffee cream
2 Tbl. sugar	3 c. sifted flour
1 yeast cake	¼ c. butter or margarine
3 egg yolks, beaten	½ tsp. salt

Add yeast and sugar to warm milk. Add cream and beaten egg yolks. Cut butter into flour and salt. Add milk and egg mixture. Blend well. Chill at least 2 hours in refrigerator. Roll out dough on lightly floured board into a rectangular shape, approximately 9x14 inches. Cut into 6 equal strips lengthwise. Twist 2 strips together, ending up with 3 twisted strips. Place the 3 twisted strips 1 inch apart on a greased baking sheet. Let rise in warm place for about 1½ hours. Bake 20 to 25 minutes at 375 degrees. When cool, ice lightly with confectioners sugar frosting.

*   *   *

GENUINE DANISH KLEINER
(Aegte Danske Klejner)

3 eggs	½ c. butter
1 c. sugar	1 tsp. baking powder
½ tsp. salt	3-4 c. flour
4 Tbl. cream	1 tsp. vanilla or cardamon

Beat eggs and sugar. Add all ingredients but flour. Stir in enough flour to make batter stiff enough to roll out like cookies. Cut in diamond shapes, make slit in center, and pull one end through slit. Cook in deep fat until light brown, cooking 6 or 8 at a time. Turn with fork. Place on brown paper to cool. (Use at least 1½ lb. shortening for frying the Kleiner in this recipe.)

*   *   *

FIRST OF THE GARDEN
(Ruskomsnusk)

Precook:
2 c. small or cubed new
   potatoes
1 c. sliced new carrots
1 c. fresh shelled peas
Add:
1 tsp. salt
1/8 tsp. pepper

Bubble together for 1 min:
2 Tbl. butter
2 Tbl. flour
1 Tbl. green onion tops

2 c. milk
Stir until thickened

Add cooked potatoes, carrots and peas. Simmer together 15 minutes.

Other variations call for:

½ c. chopped ham
   or bacon
½ c. carrots
½ c. peas
½ c. potatoes

½ c. turnips
2 Tbl. parsley
1 onion
½ c. celery

This recipe was used by two of the original families of this Trufant community. However, the Danish cook books generally indicate the second variation. This is a combination of vegetables from the first garden harvest, but the second variation calls for vegetables not generally available at early harvest. Frozen baby peas may be used with the new carrots and potatoes.

BREAD SOUP
(Brodsuppe)

8 slices pumpernickle   ½ lemon
1 stick cinnamon   1 c. fruit juice

Cut bread into cubes and soak in water to cover overnight. Cook until mushy and put through a colander. Return to kettle adding cinnamon, juices, lemon and sugar to taste. Heat and serve with whipped cream. Canned plums may be substituted for fruit juice.

*   *   *

HOLIDAY FRUIT SOUP
(Fin Sodsuppe for Sondag)

1 c. sugar   ½ tsp. salt
1 c. prunes   ½ orange
1 c. raisins   ½ lemon
½ c. tapioca   3 apples
2 sticks cinnamon   3 peaches
½ c. sago

Let eight cups water come to boil, add sugar and salt. Gradually add sago. Add prunes and raisins. Cut orange and lemon in small pieces, pare apples and dice them, pare peaches and cut in pieces. Add cut up fruit and cinnamon sticks to water mixture and boil slowly for about 1 hour. May be served hot or cold with croutons. To shorten cooking period, let ½ c. of sago soak in ½ c. of cold water for a few minutes before adding to liquid. This attractive holiday soup may also be served as a dessert.

*   *   *

All Aboard for Wiarton

There wasn't anything outwardly "ethnic" about the old neighborhood on the Northwest side of Detroit where I grew up in the 1930s. You could scour the streets for days without seeing a fez, a turban, a beret, a mysterious olive-skinned senorita in a black mantilla, or even an old grandmother in a babushka.

Violins might sigh in dimly lighted cabarets in other parts of the city, where the streets were redolent with the spicy aromas of foreign cooking. But if you lived in the vicinity of Grand River and West Grand Boulevard, you had to satisfy yourself with home cooking at "Mom's Restaurant." And you'd better like stewed chicken with dumplings or well done roast beef with mashed potatoes, because that's where the entrees stopped.

Ethnic? No, we weren't ethnic at all. We dressed like Americans. We spoke English. Our fathers all worked for Ford Motor Company, and drove Ford cars. Our mothers were housewives and didn't drive at all.

Of course, we always spent our summer vacations and long holiday weekends with relatives in Canada. And therein lies the difference.

Like most other nationality groups, Canadians tended to stick together after they left their native soil and settled in big cities "south of the border." Just as the Poles staked out Hamtramck and the Hungarians claimed Del Ray, Canadians carved out their own enclaves in the Motor City where they could live and work with their fellow ex-patriots.

Economics probably was the biggest reason for the massive migration from Canada to Detroit in the early 1900s. With the birth of the auto industry, Detroit offered thousands upon thousands of jobs at unheard of pay rates in its fast-multiplying factories.

By Robert Clock

Canadians, many of whom were only one or two generations removed from the British Isles, were quick to realize the advantages of resettling again in the United States, particularly when their Canadian roots weren't all that deep.

Immigration laws were fairly easy to live with in the early days of the century. Many Canadians simply moved across the border, found jobs and began voting as U.S. citizens. Others went through the process of naturalization to legalize their new status. Still others lived and worked in the United States but still claimed Canadian citizenship.

It wasn't until World War II that immigration officials made a serious effort to straighten out the mess. Some Canadians who refused to change their citizenship were deported. Others, including my mother, were granted derivative citizenship because their forebears at one time or another had become U.S. citizens. The remainder were naturalized by the courts after boning up on American history and swearing to support the U.S. Constitution.

While most second generation Poles and Hungarians probably will never see the land of their origins, nearby Canada was familiar territory to all the kids in my neighborhood. Allan Murch had relatives in Montreal and the flinty mining towns of northern Quebec. Mike Portlance had an uncle living on a farm near Ottawa. Fred Shaw's folks had emigrated from Brigden, Ontario, a tiny farming community south of Sarnia.

My mother was born at Oxenden, Ontario, and I had countless uncles, aunts and cousins scattered like skipping stones along the south shore of Colpoy Bay, a long arm of Georgian Bay that slices like a fjord across the Bruce Peninsula. Although the area is a scant 240 miles north of Detroit, the precipitous limestone escarpments of the Bruce Peninsula make it a different world from the flood plains of the Detroit area.

When I was a boy, a trip to Oxenden was like a journey backward in time, since such citified improvements as electricity, running water and indoor plumbing were still some years in the future for much of rural Canada. It was an exciting experience for a city boy to drive home a herd of cows in the evening, help with the milking, and turn a cream separator by the light of a kerosene lantern until his arms ached.

It was also fun to hang around my Uncle John's sawmill, which was powered by the rushing waters of Gleason Creek which empties into Colpoy Bay at Oxenden. Uncle John had narrow gauge railroad tracks running from the mill into the yard where he stored his lumber. A kid could spend all day riding the little cars like scooters in and out of the mill and around the lumber yard.

Sometimes Aunt Mary, Uncle John's wife, would hitch up Old Bud, her Indian pony, to the democrat and take all the kids on a day's outing. We usually stopped for a picnic lunch at Bruce's Cave --- a huge, black hole in the face of the limestone escarpment above the bay. Then we would spend the afternoon picking raspberries which Aunt Mary would convert into pies, jams, and preserves.

Although summer trips to Oxenden were idyllic, winter excursions into that awesome landscape were more adventurous because they had to be made by rail. Highways weren't reliable that far north in the wintertime. I usually made the trip alone the day after Christmas, leaving Detroit about 10 p.m. from the Grand Trunk station and immediately crossing the Detroit River to Windsor, Ontario, aboard a car ferry. Two hours later, after a good deal of shunting back and forth, the train would pull out of the Windsor station. If you were lucky there'd be a vendor aboard with a reed basket packed with salmon sandwiches, apples and candy bars.

Northbound travelers had a two-hour layover at the London station in the middle of the night. Then, just before daybreak, a caravan of some of the oldest coaches in the stable of the Canadian National Railroad would lurch out of the station behind an ancient steam locomotive. Coal oil lamps suspended from the ceiling of the coaches would sway ominously as we crossed the high wooden trestle at St. Marys and pitched forward through the winter dawn toward Stratford and points north.

The train stopped at every station along the way and there was always time in those unhurried days to disembark and sample the cuisine of the station restaurant. It was at these outposts that I developed a fondness for raisin pie, which runs a close second to butter tarts as Canada's national dessert.

Early in the afternoon, the train would reach Park Head where a combination baggage car and coach heated by a wood stove was waiting to pick up passengers bound for Wiarton, a metropolis of 5,000 at the base of the Bruce Peninsula. An hour later amid great clouds of hissing steam we would arrive at the Wiarton station where Aunt Mary and Old Bud would be waiting with the cutter.

Although many families owned automobiles, sleighs and cutters were the most common mode of winter transportation on the unplowed roads of the Bruce Peninsula well into the 1940s.

I would stow my suitcase under the seat of the cutter and then slide under the lap robe next to Aunt Mary. Within seconds we would be whistling along the snowy shore road toward Oxenden, three miles distant, with sleigh bells keeping time to the hollow clip-clop of Old Bud's hoofs. I have traveled in many kinds of conveyances since then, including bullet trains and transcontinental airliners, but I have never experienced such a sensation of pure speed as I did in the cutter behind Old Bud.

Chrismas week always went too fast. I remember best the multi-course breakfasts Aunt Mary used to conjure up on the huge wood range in her steamy kitchen; long hours on snowshoes covering trap lines with my cousin; bob-sledding with village kids down the steep hill behind the mill; hearty suppers in the light of kerosene lamps with my farm cousins; bone-cold bedrooms, but warm beds heated with sadirons from the top of the kitchen range.

For months afterward, I would make mental excursions back to the wintry shores of Colpoy Bay, where life was tailor-made for a hopelessly romantic teen-age boy.

BUTTER TARTS

Visit any bakery in Ontario or Quebec and chances are pretty good you'll end up buying butter tarts, or tartlettes de le beurre, because they look so good. And yet they are virtually unknown on the American side of the border, except among folks of Canadian extraction. Bakery butter tarts are made and sold in little aluminum cups, which we usually wash and save so we can make more tarts when we get home. Shallow muffin tins work almost as well.

Prepare 20 tart shells using your favorite pie crust recipe. Combine in a mixing bowl:

2 eggs	Pinch of salt
2 c. brown sugar	2 tsp. vanilla
3 Tbl. butter	A few walnuts and raisins

Beat until bubbly and fill tart shells ½ to 2/3 full. Bake in a hot oven 10 to 12 minutes.

*   *   *

TOMATO BUTTER

It is difficult to put Tomato Butter in any particular culinary category. It may be served as a relish with roast beef, but it's also delicious spread on bread and butter.

5 lb. tomatoes	½ tsp. cloves
½ qt. vinegar	½ tsp. allspice
1½ lb. white sugar	½ tsp. cinnamon
½ tsp. red pepper	½ tsp. salt

Peel and soak the tomatoes in the vinegar and sugar for 2 hours. Prepare a small bag with the spices sewn into it and add it to the tomatoes. Boil the mixture until thick, about 3 hours, stirring occasionally to prevent scorching. Pour into small sterile jars and seal immediately with paraffin.

By Robert Clock

SOUR CREAM RAISIN PIE

Unless you own your own cows and sour your own cream, you cannot duplicate the sour cream raisin pie I remember from my early trips to Canada. However, the following recipe using butter- milk instead of sour cream comes very close to the real thing - with far fewer calories. Canadians prefer light raisins, but either light or dark may be used.

1 c. raisins	1 c. buttermilk
2 eggs (separated)	1 Tbl. flour
1 c. sugar	1 tsp. vanilla

Cover raisins with water and cook until raisins plump. Drain well. Stir other ingredients (except egg whites) over low heat until smooth and thick. Stir in drained raisins. Pour into a baked 9-inch pie crust. For meringue topping, beat the 2 remaining egg whites until stiff and add one Tbl. sugar. Spread meringue over pie and bake at 350 degrees until peaks are browned. Serve cool.

*   *   *

GREEN STEWED TOMATOES

Because Canada is located so far north and summers are so short, tomatoes sometimes take forever to ripen. That is why green tomato recipes have become so popular among Canadians. My mother used to serve green stewed tomatoes in little dessert dishes along with the main course.

5-6 large green tomatoes	2 slices white bread
1 large onion	Salt and pepper to taste

Peel and stem tomatoes after dunking in scalding water. Cut into pieces. Slice onions into fairly stout rings. Cook in a saucepan with a very small amount of water until tomatoes and onions are ten- der. Before serving, remove the crusts from 2 slices of white bread and break the bread in small pieces into tomatoes. Add salt and pep- per to taste. If calories are no problem, 1 Tbl. butter enhances the flavor.

POACHED FINNAN HADDIE

If there is one distinctive aroma I remember from boyhood it is the heady vapors arising from a skillet of finnan haddie poaching on the kitchen range. Originally a product of Scotland, this smoked and brined haddock is popular throughout Ontario and is beginning to win favor in the United States. Although it used to be a poor man's dish, you would never know it by the prices demanded for it today.

2 lb. finnan haddie	1 bay leaf
1 slice lemon	2 peppercorns
Water	

Rinse haddie, then place all ingredients in a skillet and poach for 20 minutes until fish is fork tender. Remove to platter garnished with lemon wedges. Serve with buttered boiled potatoes, a green vegetable and great chunks of home-made white bread.

*　　　　　*　　　　　*

CANADIAN SPAGHETTI

If a common thread ran through the Canadian-American families living in Detroit during the Depression, it was the fact that most of them served a dish that we kids called "Canadian Spaghetti." It is filling, inexpensive and really quite tasty for a meatless dish. Sometimes my mother would serve grated cheddar cheese as a garnish.

12 oz. spaghetti	1 large onion, sliced
1 large can tomatoes, sliced	Salt and pepper to taste
1 green pepper, sliced	

Cook spaghetti according to package, then cook vegeatables until tender and liquid is almost gone. Toss with spaghetti and return to burner for a minute or two until excess moisture is absorbed and spaghetti is steamy. Serve immediately with tossed salad and hot garlic bread.

PRINCE OF WALES CAKE

If you liked the way cakes used to taste before the era of packaged mixes, then you'll love Prince of Wales cake. It is a substantial, matter-of-fact cake with lots of fruit and nuts in it. But it stops short of being a real fruit cake. The following recipe has been in our family almost 80 years, having been brought form England to Canada by a friend of my grandfather. Because it is fussier to make than a mix, we use it mostly on birthdays. For picnics we make it as a sheet cake in a 9x13 pan and eliminate the lemon filling.

1½ c. white sugar	3 c. sifted all-purpose flour
¾ c. butter	1½ tsp. baking soda
3 eggs	1½ tsp. cream of tarter
3 Tbl. molasses	1½ tsp. cinnamon
¼ c. lemon juice and/or	1½ c. raisins
grated peel of ½ lemon	½ c. chopped walnuts
1 c. sour cream or	
buttermilk	

Cream together the sugar and butter. Add .the rest of the ingredients (except raisins and walnuts) and beat until smooth. Stir in the nuts and walnuts. Bake at 350 degrees in 2 greased and floured pans, about 45-60 minutes, or until pick comes out clean.

Filling:

1 egg	Juice of 1 lemon
½ c. sugar	1 Tbl. cold water

Let come to a boil and stir for 2-3 minutes. Put filling between cool layers of cake and frost with butter cream frosting or dust with powdered sugar.

*   *   *

PEAR CONSERVE

Pears are always a problem. They ripen all at once and there are too many of them. Your friends and neighbors will accept only so many grocery bags bulging with pears before they start avoiding you on the street. Pear conserve helps solve the problem. It is delicious on your morning toast and small jars make attractive Christmas gifts.

A sufficient number of   1 whole lemon
   pears to leave 5 lb. pulp   5 lb. sugar
3 whole oranges

Remove seeds from oranges and lemon and put them through food grinder with pears. Place in preserving kettle with sugar and simmer until mixture thickens when allowed to cool on a spoon. Pour into sterile jelly jars. Seal with paraffin.

*   *   *

SHORT BREAD

This old favorite is easy to make and melts in your mouth. Canadians often include short bread in their boxes of Christmas cookies, but it is delicious any season of the year. Although butter imparts a better flavor, short bread also may be made with your favorite margarine.

Soften: 1 c. butter at room temperature.

Sift: 1 c. all-purpose flour   ½ c. corn starch
       ½ c. powdered sugar   a pinch of salt

Sift twice and mix with softened butter. Pat into cookie sheet and bake in 250 degree oven for 10-15 minutes. Watch very closely. Short bread is done when it begins to turn brown at the edges. Slice into 2-inch diamonds or squares while still warm. For a more piquent taste, add up to ½ tsp. lemon or almond flavoring to dough.

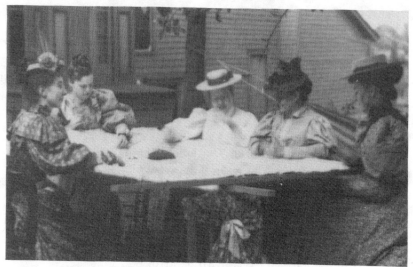

Ten hands always worked better than two when it came to quilting. And, in the days before TV, quilting was a social activity for women. Cooped up indoors during the long winters, isolated by winter and distance, women welcomed the chance to get together to chat, gossip and -- not incidently -- quilt. Also, when quilts are streched out on their frames, they can be cumbersome and take up a whole room. Few families had the kind of space to spare to give a quilt a room of its own while the wife pecked away at it for months. It was much easier and faster to gather together neighbors and friends for the task.

The quilting bee gave women a chance to exchange patterns or try out the new one sent by Cousin Maudie from Buffalo. Women took pride in their artistic ability to arrange blocks of material into beautiful designs. In addition, they were given a chance to show off their needlework skills by taking the tiniest stitches possible in the intricate scroll and spiral designs.

And attending a quilting bee for a bride-to-be must have been the forerunner of our showers today. Somehow the personal touch of the quilt seems lovlier than plastic dishpans or acrylic cutting boards.

The Old-Time Finnish Sauna

The Finnish sauna, like almost everything else, was different in the old days. I'm afraid the patrons of the modern steam-baths wouldn't even recognize the oldtimers.

When the Old Country Finns poured into the Upper Michigan wilderness, the first thing they usually built was a sauna. They lived it it while the homestead cabin was being built.

The sauna was a small log hut with one door, one window, and one airhole. The stove, or heater, was made out of special stones that wouldn't crack from the heat. There was no chimney. The smoke poured into the sauna and out of the airhole high on the wall. When the heat had risen to an infernal degree, the fire was allowed to go out, the airhole was plugged with a big rag, and it was ready for bathing. The black on the walls did not rub off on your skin.

Usually a great big pot of water sat permanently on the rocks of the "kiuas." A wooden tub of cold water sat on the floor near the door. Cedar switches were laid on the bench or in the cold water tub. There were no "birchers" in our area, but some do prefer the birch switches. Several steps led up to the platform where you could lie down and relax. Smaller tubs and pans were placed upside down on a bench. On a little shelf on the wall you could find a kitchen brush and yellow laundry soap. There was no dressing room in the oldtime sauna. In the summer you simply left your dirty clothes outside by the door, usually on a bench, but in the winter time you dropped them on a bench right in the suana. However, you couldn't bring your clean clothes in because of the dampness. After you steamed yourself, spanked yourself with a cedar switch until you tingled from

By Jingo Viitala Vachon

Reprinted by permission from "Tall Timber Tales -- Sketches and Stories" by Jingo Viitala Vachon, copright 1973 by L'Anse Sentinel and R. J. Cristison.

head to foot, and scrubbed yourself until every groove and pore in your skin was scraped, you dumped pails of water over your head, flushing away the week's accumulation of dead skin and soap suds. Then you simply picked up your dirty clothes and walked into the house in the altogether. The old country Finns thought nothing of this. It was a way of life. When so-called outlanders began coming in, they were terribly shocked. They simply couldn't understand that to the Finns, nudity and cleanliness went together; sex belonged in a bedroom.

Our neighboring farmer was a gentle little old man. He was barely over five feet tall, and his wife was smaller than he was. They were deeply religious and really lived their religion. They were both the kindest, gentlest, most generous old people I ever knew. Their home was always open to everybody. Drunks and fallen girls got a new lease on life there. We called them Uncle Pekka and Aunt Katri.

The new school teacher was an Irish colleen and had never been around Finns. Everything was a little strange to her. She was a spunky little girl and willing to learn. She began by visiting a few of the homesteaders to show she was friendly. It worked. People took to her immediately.

One Saturday night, the young daughter of the people she was boarding with arranged a visit between the teacher and this very special couple. Uncle Pekka spoke quite a bit of English, which was rather rare among the older Finns. Aunt Katri met them at the door with a stream of Finnish, and the teacher listened to the translations her friend swiftly relayed. Finally she understood that Uncle Pekka was in the sauna and would be in very shortly, and they would all have coffee and lunch together.

About fifteen minutes later, the door opened and little Uncle Pekka walked in pink and bright eyed. His clothes and his towel were draped over his arm, and he was stark naked except for his boots. He nodded to the teacher, and with a pleasant "Goot Eefning" he dropped his dirty clothes in the corner by the door and walked unconcerned into the bedroom. The teacher sat staring into space, not saying anything. Later she said she went blind and deaf and dumb.

In a little while Uncle Pekka walked back into the kitchen all dressed up and ready for coffee. Little Aunt Katri had outdone herself with the finest coffee bread and cake, baked special for the teacher. But the poor guest never tasted anything she was eating. I guess it took the rest of the weekend to bring her out of shock. But she really had spunk. She proved it by marrying a Finn! She took to the sauna like a duck to water, but never adapted to complete neighborly nudity. Between her Irish wit and his quiet good nature, they had a fine marriage and ten little redheads who argued in Finnish.

When I was a child, the Saturday night sauna was a family

Mrs. Mary Kangas, who came to the Copper Country from Finland in the 1890s, weaved on her homemade loom when she was 75-years-old. She learned the craft as a child in Finland. *(Photo from Michigan State Photo Archives)*

affair, and after Mother and Father scrubbed us off with the yellow laundry soap and kitchen brush, we were rinsed off and told to run into the house. Summer or snowstorm, we would run round and round the sauna, hip deep through drifts in winter, then along the icy hog-back path to the warm, big kitchen where we'd burst in glowing and breathless, but not chilled.

To the Finns, the sauna was an absolute necessity. It served many purposes. You went in after a day of exhausting labor and sweated out your weariness along with the grime. You came out relaxed and refreshed. You went in with a bad cold or the flu, sipped a bottle of whisky and sweated out the fever. It was wonderful for arthritis, rheumatism, and various aches and pains. In many cases the mothers bore their babies in the sauna. In winter it was warm, almost delivery room antiseptic after being scrubbed and scalded, there was more privacy where the family had many children, and there was oodles and oodles of hot water.

The Finns have been known throughout history as being a tough, hardy race. Perhaps the sauna had something to to with it. They are known for being natural nudists, yet their morality and clean living is among the highest in the world. To the Finns, development of the human body and mind is synonymous. A healthy body and a healthy mind produces athletes with brains and intellectuals with healthy bodies who live longer and can serve better. They see the beauty in a healthy body as they see the architecture of Saarinen, the sculpture of Aaltonen, or the stirring music of Sibelius. Their presidents have been known to swim regularly among the ice cakes through the biting Finnish winter, and Finland's Tapio Rautavaara, (or Johnny Cash), folk singer-actor, was a winner in the Olympics -- a decathlon champ. However, this is only a hint....

Sometimes I think the incomparable Finnish "Sisu," which I call sheer, unadulterated, tenacious bull-headedness, was born in the infernal heat of a primitive sauna where they were tested for endurance. It makes me sad to see the modern private bathrooms take the place of the family bathing I knew as a child. We had a much healthier attitude toward nudity, and although we thought Father looked silly in his saggy baggy underwear, he just looked like Father in the altogether.

When my father came to this country, one of the first things he saw on a New York street was a group of men whistling and hooting at a girl who lifted her skirt enough to expose her laced shoe top as she stepped off a curb and over a puddle. He thought they were retarded. It wasn't until later that he found out what had excited the street corner Lotharios.

Perhaps I belong to a different breed of people, but I think if more kids had been raised to view the human body as a natural, healthy, everyday sort of thing, we wouldn't have men and boys popping their eyeballs at mini skirts or shorty shorts, or hiding nudie photos under mattresses, or going ga-ga over nudie films, or having girls simply die of embarrassment the first time they have to bathe a male during nurses' training, or ladies having traumatic shocks at the sight of a man without britches.

Most important of all, the impact of sexy advertising would be cut down considerably, pornography sales would go down, and I bet you my bottom dollar that skirts would lengthen in cold weather!

Since the sauna has become universally accepted and quite popular among non-Finns, I would like to say that the funniest thing about these people is that although they go in for family bathing, most of them leave their bathing suits on! How in Sam Hill can you scrub up in a bathing suit? A wrap-around towel, maybe, but bathing suits, good grief!

FINNISH GINGER SNAP

Cream together 1 c. oleo and 1 c. sugar. Add 2 beaten eggs and stir. Mix in ½ c. molasses. Sift together 4½ c. flour, 3 tsp. ginger, 1 tsp. salt and 1 tsp. soda. Stir into above mixture. Let stand in refrigerator overnight. Roll out thin on lightly floured board and cut with a cookie cutter.

Bake at 400 degrees for about 15 minutes. Makes 30.

*   *   *

TURNIP CASSEROLE
(Finnish Lanttulaatikko)

2½ c. boiled turnips (mashed)	1½ Tbl. sugar
4 Tbl. butter	2 eggs, beaten
1½ tsp. salt	1¼ c. bread crumbs
	1/8 tsp. pepper

Combine all ingredients except ¼ c. bread crumbs. Spoon into oiled casserole; top with remaining crumbs. Bake at about 350 degrees for 30 minutes or until brown on top.

*   *   *

FINNISH BREAD
(Rieska)

2 c. flour	1 tsp. baking powder
½ c. barley flour	1 tsp. soda
1 tsp. salt	1 c. buttermilk
1 tsp. sugar	

Mix and form into round ball and flatten out. Bake 15 minutes at 375 degrees. Brush with oleo after baking.

By Elma Ranta

APPLE SUGAR CAKE
(Omena Sokerikakku)

¼ c. margarine
1 c. sugar
2 eggs
2 c. sifted flour
1½ tsp. baking powder
Dash of salt

¾ c. light cream
2 apples, peeled, cored and sliced
Cinnamon sugar (2 Tbl. sugar mixed with 1 tsp. cinnamon)

Cream the butter and sugar together until thick and lemon colored. Add the eggs, beating until light. Sift the flour with the baking powder and salt, and add alternately to the batter with the cream. Mix until the batter is smooth. Pour into a well greased 9x12 inch pan and insert the apple slices so that the outer edges are up. Sprinkle evenly with the cinnamon sugar.

Bake at 350 degrees for about 50 minutes or until a toothpick comes out clean.

* * *

BLUEBERRY SOUP
(Mustikkakiisseli)

2 c. water
2 c. fresh or frozen blueberries
1 stick cinnamon or ½ tsp. lemon juice

3 Tbl. sugar
3 Tbl. corn starch
3 Tbl. cold water
Whipped cream

Bring the 2 c. of water to a boil in a saucepan and add the blueberries, sugar and cinnamon or lemon juice. Add the cornstarch to the 3 Tbl. of cold water and mix into a smooth paste. When the berries have cooked about 10 minutes, slowly stir in cornstarch mixture into the boiling soup. Cook 2 more minutes or until clear and thickened. Cool and serve chilled with whipped cream on top.

CABBAGE ROLLS
(Kaalikaaryleet)

1 large head of cabbage	½ tsp. allspice
2 tsp. salt	1 lb. of ground lean beef
Water	1½ c. cooked rice or pearl
½ c. cream	barley
½ c. fresh bread crumbs	½ c. dark corn syrup
1 tsp. salt	2 c. boiling water

Cut the core out of the cabbage and place the head in salted boiling water in a large pot. As the outer leaves of the cabbage become tender, peel them off. Let cool.

In a bowl, mix together well the cream, bread crumbs, ½ c. water, 1 tsp. salt, allspice and ground beef. Add the cooked rice or barley. Place 1 or 2 Tbl. of the filling on each cabbage leaf. Wrap the leaf around the filling on each cabbage leaf and tuck in the ends.

Place the rolls seam side down in a buttered casserole, and drizzle the corn syrup over them (brush the rolls lightly to distribute the syrup evenly). Cover and bake in a hot oven (400 degrees) for 20 minutes, then remove the cover and pour about 2 c. boiling water or enough to almost cover the rolls. Leave the casserole uncovered, lower heat to 350 degrees, and continue baking for 1 hour. Serve hot. Makes about 12 to 16 rolls.

*   *   *

FINNISH OVEN PANCAKES

1 qt. milk	1 c. flour
3 eggs	salt
½ c. sugar	nutmeg

Melt heaping Tbl. butter in 9x12 inch pans. Whip eggs, add milk and sugar, then flour and salt. Then pour in hot pans and sprinkle nutmeg on top of batter. Bake 40 minutes at 450 degrees. Serve hot.

Before the Devil Knows Yer Dead

It was not land but jobs that first beckoned Irish immigrants into the Michigan wilderness. A proud, hard-working people, they were often exploited and denied jobs in the settled eastern cities. "No Irish Need Apply" signs posted in employment offices were a curse to these new immigrants.

So they fled to the nation's interior, to Michigan. From the mining camps of the state's northern-most reaches, to the Irish quarters of Detroit, these people not long from the Emerald Isle found hope and a glimmer of prosperity to come.

The Irish also made their way to one of Michigan's countless lumber boom towns, Hubbardston. As it was more than a century ago, the village remains today a reminder of why the Irish came to Michigan, and why their children's children settled here as well.

Nestled in a river valley in northeastern Ionia County, this village of 1,200 souls is a "wee bit of Mother Ireland" transplanted. The Catholic Church built on a hilltop remains the pulse of the community's Irish ancestry. The great-grandsons and great-granddaughters of the immigrants -- the Feyans, the O'Malleys, the McGinns -- are still here.

Nowhere do the roots of the Old Country run deeper than in Shiels' Tavern, the traditional watering hole for generations of the town's Irish-Americans, and not by coincidence, the oldest licensed tavern in Michigan.

In 1878, Terence Shiels opened the doors to his tavern for the first time. Then a prospering lumber town, Hubbardston was liberally populated with saloons. Shiels' was hardly keen competition for the dozen or more saloons scattered along main street.

By Mark Nixon

But as the logging heyday faded, so did Hubbardston's taverns experience an abrupt demise. But Terence Shiels and his sparsely-furnished tavern thrived. Undoubtedly, Shiels' Tavern has been silent witness to countless wedding receptions, wakes, St. Patrick's Day celebrations, as well as an occasional rowdy Saturday night.

Employing the heaviest Irish brogue, a visitor to this Irish pub once wrote: "Those were the days, lad. A bucket o' beer would set a man back but a thin doyme. The Cunninghams and Cahalens were down to Terry Shiels, rubbin' elbows, the blarney flowin' free as Irish Mist. There would be Knuckles O'Toole playin' sweet strains on the upright piano, enough to make a grown man cry. Into the wee hours we'd be singin' and weavin' out the door, and sure as I'm standin' here, one o' the boys would shout, 'May you be in heaven three hours before the devil knows yer dead!' "

Because it thrived both in prosperity and hard times, Shiels' is a monument to the Irish immigrant. Nor are the village folks of present times forgetting their heritage. Every St. Patrick's Day, the entire town turns out for some form of celebration. Shiels' is the 'meeting hall' for that too. In 1968, Hubbardston celebrated its centennial, and the celebrants took to the streets for days-long revelry. "One young lass rode a horse through the front door of Shiels' and then rode it out the back," one villager recalls. "The streets were so full of beer bottles they used a pickup truck and scoop shovels to clean up. The cops were swarming the town, but," he added with a smile, "there was no trouble at all."

How the Irish came to settle in Hubbardston – and for that matter, Michigan – is a story of despair and triumph. To better understand that story, it is necessary to briefly retrace the history of Mother Ireland, the country that gave the world Yeats and Joyce, the Emerald Isle.

Various Celtic tribes inhabited this land more than 500 years before Christ. Eventually, one tribe of Celts dominated, the Gaels. They are the direct ancestors of the Irish people we know today. The Gaels also gave us the country's name, which comes from the name of a Celtic princess, Eire.

Another name virtually synonymous with Ireland is St. Patrick. Born more than 400 years after Christ, he was a Roman citizen living in what today is England. As a youth, he was captured in one of the endless tribal wars and taken as a slave to Eire-land. Undaunted by this fate, he rose to a position of high esteem, and spread the word of Christianity. By 432 A.D. Ireland was considered Christianized.

Much as it was among the clans of Scotland, the family of medieval Ireland was the dominant social unit. So it remains today among Irish, some say. "Gaelic devotion to family origins is perhaps this people's most primal trait," writes one Irish historian.

Throughout the centuries, kinsmen were consigned by birth to one of three stations in life: aristocrats, serfs and specialized groups professing some needed culture or trade.

It was the peasantry that gave us many of the traditional Irish foods we know today: boxty, nettle soup, colcannon and stirabout. Inhabitants along Ireland's mountainous coastline dined on other well-known Irish cooking, including trout, salmon, cockles and the famous prawns of Dublin Bay.

The Irish also concocted honey and wine to make mead, probably the grandfather to Ireland's premiere liqueur, Irish Mist. They were also inventors of whiskey, which in old Gaelic dialect means "water of life".

AN OLD IRISH TOAST

Health and long life to you,
Land without rent to you,
A child every year to you,
And may you die in Ireland.

It was one knobby-shaped tuber, though, that became both the salvation and ruination of the Irish peasant class. The fate that befell the humble potato was the catalyst which uprooted the Irish from their homeland and pointed them in the direction of the New Country, America.

The potato was introduced to Ireland in 1587 by the English nobleman-explorer, Sir Walter Raleigh. Well-suited to the climate, the potato thrived in Ireland and became an indispensable part of the

Irish diet. Potatoes were praised in song and verse, and were more often than not a part of every meal: boxty (similar to potato cakes) for breakfast, donegal pies for dinner, Irish stew for supper.

Despite shortages of available farmland, the English conquest of the 17th century, rebellions, the Irish peasant could count on the life-sustaining potato.

So it was until the early decades of the 1800s. After repeated crop failures, there came the Great Potato Famine of 1845. Ravaged by blight, vast crops of potatoes became little more than rotting, malformed bits of pulp. In successive years the blight worsened. People starved. It is estimated that a million people died in Ireland as a result of the famine.

Another million fled the home land in hopes of finding a brighter tomorrow in North America. On the night before their departure, it was not uncommon for these desperate people to hold an "American Wake". It was a half-festive, half-tragic farewell from those who remained behind to those fleeing the famine.

Safe passage to Canada and the United States was no certain thing. Steerage conditions were abominable, and many died of ship fever and typhus.

After weeks of the tortuous ocean voyage, the new immigrants set foot on American soil in such ports as Quebec, Boston and New York. Too often, they were shuffled off to shanty towns where immigrants who preceded them lived in squalor, many without jobs or hopes of readily finding them. The Irish were thought to be a threat to the livelihood of those already established here, many recent immigrants themselves.

Was this the Promised Land?, Irish families asked themselves.

Bewildered, disenchanted, they gradually took stock of their situation. Eventually they would become prominent tradesmen and businessmen while their political clout became legend. These things would take time, however.

Meanwhile, the lure of far-off western frontiers caused others to uproot once more. They heard of distant lands where jobs abounded. Great railroads and canals were being built, iron and copper were being mined, logging camps were springing up overnight. All this in a place called Michigan.

IRISH COFFEE

1 jigger, Irish whiskey	1½ tsp. sugar
Hot, strong black coffee	1 Tbl. whipped cream

Heat a stemmed goblet. Add sugar and enough coffee to dissolve the sugar. Stir well. Add Irish whiskey and fill the goblet to within an inch of the brim with hot coffee. Top with whipped cream. Do not stir in the whipped cream. The true flavor comes from drinking the hot coffee and whiskey through the coolness of the cream. Makes 1 serving.

*   *   *

BOXTY BREAD

Raw potatoes, peeled	Salt
Cooked and mashed potatoes	Flour

Grate the peeled, raw potatoes. Combine an equal amount of raw and cooked potatoes. Lightly sprinkle with salt. Then add just enough flour to make a pliable dough. Knead well and roll out on a lightly floured board. Drop tablespoonfuls of dough onto a hot griddle. Cook slowly until golden brown.

Boxty became a staple of Irish life during the Great Potato Famine, 1845-1849. During those impoverished years, smaller, blighted potatoes were salvaged for the dinner table by mixing them with flour; thus, boxty. Boxty was made into an endless variety of dishes, including pancakes and dumplings. The 19th century Irish also made Pratie Cakes (prata is Irish for potato), which are nearly identical to boxty bread.

Potatoes were introduced to Ireland by Sir Walter Raleigh in 1587. Ideally suited to Ireland's climate, they became the staple of the Irish's daily diet. Many a folk ballad was sung in praise of the mighty potato, and more than one Irishman was given to say: "Be eating one potato, peeling a second, have a third in your fist and your eye on the fourth."

By Mark Nixon

WICKLOW PANCAKES

4 eggs	½ tsp. chopped thyme
2 c. milk	1 Tbl. butter
2 c. breadcrumbs	Salt
6 scallions, chopped finely	Pepper

Beat the eggs. Add breadcrumbs, milk, scallions and herbs. Season with salt and pepper. Melt butter on a griddle. When griddle is hot, pour pancake-size portion of the mixture. Reduce heat slightly. When pancake is firm on top, turn and brown on other side. Serve with a pat of butter on top. Makes 4 servings.

*   *   *

IRISH STEW

3 lb. lamb chops, fat, bone and gristle removed	1 pt. cold water
	Salt
	Pepper
6-8 potatoes, peeled	1 Tbl. chopped parsley and
4-6 medium onions	thyme, mixed

Cut chops into fairly large pieces. Place in saucepan. Arrange potatoes and onions on the chops (traditionally, potatoes and onions are left whole in Irish stew). Add water, sprinkle with salt and pepper. Add parsley and thyme. Cover and cook over low heat for about 2 hours, or cook in oven at 325 degrees for 2-2½ hours. Thicken gravy, if desired. Makes 4 servings.

Real Irish stew was made from kid, not mutton (the Irish felt their sheep too valuable to use their meat regularly at the dinner table). Potatoes were peeled for stews but otherwise left in their skins. The stew was cooked in a bastable oven, a large iron pot suspended over the smoldering embers of a turf fire. The stew was usually very thick in consistency, and was often served with pickled red cabbage.

BARM BRACK

4 c. sifted flour	1¼ c. lukewarm milk
3 Tbl. sugar	2 eggs, well beaten
½ tsp. salt	1 c. sultanas (seedless white
½ tsp. nutmeg	grapes)
2½ Tbl. butter	½ c. currants
1 pkg. yeast	¼ c. candied mixed peel, chopped

Sift together the flour, 2 Tbls. of sugar, salt, cinnamon and nutmeg. Add the butter, blending it in with a pastry blender. Dissolve yeast in ¼ c. of lukewarm milk. Combine yeast-milk mixture with the remaining milk and the egg. Stir into flour mixture until resulting mixture is smooth and elastic (about 10 minutes). Mix in fruit. Turn into a greased 8x3 inch round cake pan or glass baking dish. Cover with a cloth and place in a warm place for rising. This takes about 2 hours. The dough should rise almost to the top of the pan. Bake at 400 degrees for about one hour (375 degrees if baking with a glass dish). Barm brack is done if it shrinks slightly from the sides of the pan, and sounds hollow when slightly tapped. Now dissolve 1 Tbl. of sugar in 2 tsp. of hot water; pour this syrup over the barm brack, and return it to the oven for a few minutes. Serve slightly warm in thick slices with butter.

Barm brack is considered to be one of the oldest traditional recipes of Ireland. Barm brack stems from the old Gaelic words, boreen brack, meaning, "speckled yeast cake".

*   *   *

ROSCOMMON APPLE PUFFS

1 Tbl. honey
3 Tbl. butter or
   margarine, melted
1 liqueur glass (1-1½ oz.)
   Irish Mist Liqueur

1 Tbl. brown sugar
6 medium cooking apples,
   peeled and cored
½ lb. puff pastry or ½ recipe
   standard pastry

Mix together honey, butter, the Irish Mist Liqueur and brown sugar. Fill cored apples with this mixture. Roll out pastry and cut into 6 squares (amount of pastry depends on the size of apples). Place an apple on each square of pastry. Dampen the edges of the pastry and bring opposite corners of it together on top of the apples. Press edges on sides and top together firmly. Prick the pastry gently on the top. Place on baking sheet. Bake at 425 degrees for 25-30 minutes, or until pastry is done. Serve warm, with lemon sauce or whipped cream if desired. Make 6 servings.

*   *   *

GUR CAKE

9 slices stale bread
¼ c. plus 2 Tbl. sifted
½ tsp. baking powder
2 tsp. mixed spice
¼ tsp. salt
½ c. brown sugar, firmly
   packed

2 Tbl. butter or margarine
¾ c. currants
1 egg, slightly beaten
1/3 c. milk
Grated rind of ½ a lemon
1 recipe standard pastry

Cover bread crumbs with cold water and let soak for 1 hour. Squeeze dry. Sift together flour, baking powder, mixed spice and salt. Add butter and blend it in with pastry blender. Stir in brown sugar, currants and lemon rind. Combine egg and milk and add with the bread to the flour mixture. Blend thoroughly.

Divide pastry dough in half; line bottom and edges of a baking pan. Spread bread mixture evenly over the pastry. Top with remaining pastry, press edges together, and cut several slits in the top of pastry. Bake at 375 degrees for about 1½ hours. Sprinkle pastry crust with sugar immediately after removing from oven. Let cool, cut into squares. Makes 2 dozen 2 inch squares. Good with ice cream.

Can You Spell Czechoslovakia?

For those of you who don't follow such things, Czechoslovakia is divided into three regions -- Bohemia, Moravia and Slovakia. Bohemia and Moravia, the north-western portions of the country, are often lumped together, while Slovakia considers itself apart in culture and, to some extent, in language. Mr. Brablec is of Moravian ancestry; Mr. Walaskay of Slovakian.

In the early 1900s, the world was bursting at the seams with a new phenomenon, the industrial revolution. Since the beginning of time men were bound geographically and culturally to their birthplaces for a lifetime. All of a sudden man had a new ally which would give him new freedom and open new opportunities. This ally was the machine and its development. In large part it was the result of American ingenuity.

This was the setting that faced the youth of Europe of that day. By word of mouth from those who went and returned, by mail from adventurous companions who had already followed the magnetic pull of the new life, groups of youth were constantly being urged to strike out for themslves; to seek new adventures and fortunes not available at home.

Meanwhile, in America, the growing industry was eagerly looking for all the workers it could get and the pay offered was beyond the wildest dreams European young people had in their homelands.

So it was in Czechoslovakia. Yet there was inner conflict; here they were surrounded by natural beauty, had responsibilities to family and friends, and had centuries of background in cultural accomplishments. However, in the course of time, individuals and groups found means to sponsor their way to the new land and to new opportunities.

Upon arriving they found the greatest barrier was language. Since they needed immediate income, they stayed away from the

By Paul Walaskay

political and professional fields, and followed the industrial or farming paths. In their chosen fields, they found other persons from Czechoslovakia and they maintained their old country cultural ties. This aided their transition in adopting a new language and new customs.

These people settled into permanent homes and raised their families and became parts of the community, which in a large part was composed of people with similar backgrounds from various parts of Europe.

Independence and self-sufficiency seemed to be the motivating forces behind family structures in those days.

My parents settled near Owosso and started their family where the advantages of both industry and living from the land were available. The first priority was to own your home, both for economic security and also to teach children about responsibility and good citizenship. Children in those days did not ask questions like, "Why am I here?". They were not trying to "find themselves." We knew why we were there -- to carry out ashes, to weed the garden, to scrub floors, to paint, to fix and on and on.

The house my parents bought was at the edge of town where small farming was permitted. It was on about five acres and had a miniature barn. My father first got a few chickens which provided fresh eggs and an occasional Sunday dinner. Then he bought a few geese, essential for making feather ticks which were invaluable in cold weather. Also, the geese provided table fare for the sumptuous holiday feasts. I well remember helping my mother pluck feathers and down from the geese and then having a quilting bee where neighborhood women would make the ticks.

As their children came along, my parents needed milk. So my dad, who wasn't about to depend on anyone else, walked twenty miles to a relative who had a full-scale farm and bought a good milk cow. That cow was like part of the family -- we had all the milk, cream, cheese and butter we could use. Being too small to milk the cow, it was my job to churn the butter.

Each spring my father would get a local farmer, who had the machinery, to plow and till an acre of ground so he could put in his crop of vegetables. In addition, we had a variety of fruit trees -- pears, apples, peaches and cherries, as well as a small vineyard with Concord grapes. My father worked in a furniture factory in town and devoted his spare time to the garden. Of course, the children had their chores in picking tomato catepillers and potato bugs off plants since we didn't have insecticides then. We kept busy weeding and thinning plants all spring and summer.

When fall came around, it was my mother's turn to shine. For weeks on end the house smelled of boiling fruit, vegetables and spices as she canned and canned. Of course, the children had some vocational education in the areas of peeling, washing, sterilzing, mashing, blending, slicing and packing. In a few weeks, all of the garden produce magically ended up in jars and glasses in the form of vegetables, fruits, relishes, pickles, juices and jellies. All winter long it was comforting to see rows and rows of food on the shelves of the pantry and fruit cellar.

My school was one-and-a-half miles walk each way. There were no buses or transportation -- also no need for elaborate gymnasiums or exercise programs. In school we learned the American way of life. My parents eagerly shared our learning since through us they learned about this new land they lived in.

Being raised by parents who were Czech was both a challenge and a pleasant experience. Even being able to spell Czechoslovakia put me a cut above the average kid in school.

My parents brought with them their traditions, customs, foods, recipes and arts and crafts. Their five children thrived and learned and lived within the social and traditional customs of my parents' background. As time went on the influence of American living blended with the ethnic background. Out of this came a generation that had a dual culture which had the advantage of each. At holidays we enjoyed the traditional as well as the contemporary food. We learned crafts and skills which my parents brought. We learned my parents language, instilling in us the idea that verbal expression has more than one dimension. In short, we were a fortunate generation to have this dual culture.

To a great degree, when the third generation came along, the old culture was pretty much pushed into the background, but when this generation became old enough to question, they started to revive interest in their family background. Since food is one cultural dimension which can be provided and shared very readily, we see a resurgance of interest within this third generation to recapture the culinary arts of their grandparents.

A Bohemian Wedding

The early Bohemian wedding in Michigan was the Mardi Gras and an earthquake combined. Though necessarily involved, the betrothed were by no means the whole cheese. To begin with, they were expected to have the foresight not to set the date which might conflict with peak periods of planting or harvest. And it ought to come during outdoor weather, too. No farm house or rural social hall could quite provide for all who'd be there.

Usually hosted by the bride's parents, the wedding celebration was a cooperative effort calling on the willing assistance of friends and relatives. It took a lot of organization and staging. Ordinarily, two ladies who were known to have a knack for doing the thing right, were sent out among the Moravians to invite them verbally and, at the same time, to suggest or get a fair notion of what they would furnish by way of milk, eggs, cream, pastry, chickens, meat and, in prohibition years, homebrew. The vagaries of straight potluck couldn't be trusted. Invitations were not printed in those days. The two specialists and a strong grapevine sufficed. Only distant guests who couldn't be reached otherwise received a letter and American neighbors were particularly welcome.

Our two ladies had another duty. They took charge of the cooking and might also be asked to see that some music would be in readiness. If the purse was thin, local accordian and horn players could be relied on. If affluence or credit were available, a semi-professional band from Toledo, Detroit, or Owosso might be called in. Of course, all of these musicians were Moravians, although after the 1930s some infiltration of other nationalities wasn't uncommon.

The first installment of the three-day solemnization opened

By Carl Brablec

with the arrival of informal committees to get the premises set up, the kitchen and pantries put in readiness, benches and chairs hauled in, refreshments stored, and the whole farmstead put on general alert. In the afternoon, the musicians were likely to arrive and the "veselka", a sort of warm-up, got under way. By early evening there was a great sense of festivity aroused among the large numbers of the advance guard. About this time there was a general scattering of the men present to their respective farms for a hurried milking of cows and a return to the proceedings at the site of festivity, by now fairly advanced.

Well-fortified against any harm from a snake bite, the first day's celebrants made it home soon after midnight to be sure of the morrow.

KOLACHE

1 pkg. yeast	3 c. flour
½ c. warm milk	2 Tbl. sugar
½ lb. butter	1 tsp. salt
3 egg yolks	

Dissolve yeast in warm milk. Beat butter and sugar together until creamy. Add egg yolks and yeast, mixing well. Add remaining ingredients, mixing thoroughly. Refrigerate overnight. Roll out and cut into circles. Put poppyseed, grated cheese, apricot or plum butter or nut filling in center of each before baking at 375 degrees for 20 minutes. When cool, sprinkle with powdered sugar.

The writer recalls a Catholic church as the most frequent site for the marriage ceremony. Now the invited guests came on to the early afternoon feast. In additon to the mounds of meat of three or four kinds, there had to be soup -- regardless of the heat of the day, soup was served. For some reasons, it belonged. Dessert was in the form of inimitable baked goods and pastries called vdolky, kolache, milosti, buchty, baleshky and struld.

Milosti was a delicate pastry covered with powdered sugar once referred to by an American as "angle wings." Most of the named delicacies were baked in a rich dough, centers filled with fruit pastes from peaches, apples, plums, dates and who knows what? Other ambrosial creations had the fruit on top, all fused with the dough in the woodfire range ovens. The two promoting ladies knew total success.

Before and after Prohibition years, alcoholic beverages were no problem other than the considerable cost for a quantity to quench so many thirsts over such a prolonged time. But like the Latin phrase "Amor Nummi" suggests, it was a time for extravagance: "all sheets to the wind" and it didn't hurt all that much right then! Prohibition compelled some concession to the Constitution of the United States. The homemade wines and brews were dispensed in the tool shed or corncrib during veselka; boldness and relaxation brought the potations closer to the action as the merriment moved into the second day. Guests were a bit more discreet with the occasional gallon of moonshine brought from an unknown source by an unknown person.

Of course, a fair number of the men, especially, might not have made it home that night. What with all the small fry gleefully sliding over the slick floor, one had to spend more time at the "bar" than dancing. An occasional farm wife got to the home place on such a night and did the unavoidable milking. The final morning found selected celebrants rousing stiffly from the back seats of open touring cars; some found the haymow hot but deliciously quiet and some of the near neighbors arrived to help with the gargantuan clean-up and restoration of order. As this got started, it occurred to someone that he "ought to have a hair of the dog that bit him last night." This was still possible, fortunately. The tables of food, though in some disarray with the goodies a bit wilted and dry, were still most worthy of a final foraging effort; also, the newlyweds, long since gone, were toasted for good measure. A gradual and subdued dispersal sprinkled with thanks and well wishing was now the beginning of the end.

Some say such a wedding did for the married couple what is

lacking in many of the quick civil unions of today. A Moravian marriage had the earnest blessing of many friends and relatives. It was big stuff. Newlyweds were likely to take the combined endorsement of most of the immediate world, as well as the pledges of the ceremony, rather seriously and to heart. The pact was well ratified.

Moravians had access to a classified column in their newspapers under the heading, "Nabidnuti k Snatku", "Offer of Marriage". The typical phrasing of an ad in this lonely hearts section might read· Honest and congenial farmer age 42, widower, two healthy daughters age 14 and 16, wishes to correspond with dilligent lady of similar age, or younger, who understands farm life. Please include photo." In one case known to the writer, such a mating call received a ready response from an eligible lady who lived on a Pennsylvania hillside. She wrote back with disarming frankness and, let's say, Joe, was somewhat concerned as he arranged for her to visit. He found himself rehearsing questions he would use in determining her fitness both as wife and farming helpmate. The intended interrogation was pretty well fixed in his mind as to her housekeeping and general management abilities but how would he know if her eyesight was good? To simply give her a page of fine print to read seemed too gauche. He turned to another stratagem – placing small needles at several somewhat inconspicuous places near the chair she would use. Joe theorized that no Moravian woman could resist picking up a "lost" needle, that is, if she saw it! Well, she passed the needle test before so much as scarcely sitting down and the two of them made out as husband and wife ever after.

The marriage was a quick, quiet civil affair and for a honeymoon they tackled the ripening grain fields on the farm.

At the big wedding celebrations, there was certain to be a game of "marias" underway in some closet or corner. A sort of hybrid card game with some aspects of both bridge and pinochle, marias was played vigorously whenever occasion allowed; quite often tne winter days were whiled away in this manner. Although bowling, golfing and other newer diversions have displaced marias considerably, the American Bohemian Club members of the third generation still know and enjoy it to this day.

HOLIDAY SAUSAGE

We serve this for breakfast at Christmas and Easter. Delicious.

5 lbs. veal, ground once	5 cloves garlic, crushed
2 tsp. caraway seed	1½ c. cold water
2 Tbl. salt	Paprika for color
1 tsp. pepper	Casings

Mix thoroughly. Let meat mixture stand for one day in refrigerator. Wash casings thoroughly. (A good way to do it is to pull them on the kitchen sink faucet, then turn on the water and slowly pull the casings off.) Stuff meat in casings. Refrigerate until ready to fry.

* * *

STUFFED GREEN PEPPER

1 lb. ground beef	4-5 green peppers
1/3 c. uncooked rice	Large can tomato juice
1 tsp. salt	Pinch of sugar

Core and wash peppers. Stuff with mixture of ground beef, uncooked rice, salt and sugar. Pour tomato juice in pan and place peppers inside. Bring tomato juice to a boil on top of the stove. Cover and simmer 2 hours.

By Ethel Walaskay

WALNUT—CINNAMON COFFEE CAKE

2 pkg. yeast	2/3 c. sugar
1½ c. potato water	1½ tsp. salt
1 c. butter	1 tsp. mace
1 c. cooked potato,	2 eggs
sieved	8 c. flour

Sprinkle yeast into ½ c. very warm potato water (save the rest of the water). Add butter to potatoes and stir until melted. Add rest of water, sugar, salt and mace to potatoes, mixing well. Stir in yeast.

Beat in eggs and 5 c. flour until smooth. Gradually stir in rest of flour, making a firm dough. Knead for 10 minutes. Place in a greased bowl, turning once to grease surface. Cover, let rise until double (about another hour).

Divide dough in half. Roll into 18x2-inch rectangle, about ½-inch thick. Spread half of the filling over dough. (Use the same filling that's in the nut cookies in the previous recipe.) Roll like a jelly roll. Pinch edges and ends of dough to seal. Place dough, seam side down, on a cookie sheet, shaping into a horseshoe. Cover dough and let rise in warm place until double (about 45 minutes).

Put dough into COLD oven and turn to 300 degrees for 15 minutes, then to 350 degrees for 30 minutes and 300 degrees for 5 minutes. Turn oven off and leave in oven for 10 minutes. (Total baking time is 1 hour.)

If desired, sprinkle with powdered sugar.

SUPER—RICH, FANTASTIC NUT COOKIES

For dough, mix together and chill overnight:

>4 c. flour
>1 lb. butter
>½ pt. sour cream

Mix together filling of:

>3 c. ground walnuts
>1 c. sugar
>2 tsp. cinnamon
>Raisins (optional)
>(If too dry, moisten with a little milk.)

Roll out dough and cut into circles. Place a dab of filling on each one and pinch edges together, forming a log that's open on each end. Bake at 350 degrees for 20 minutes. Sprinkle with powdered sugar when cool.

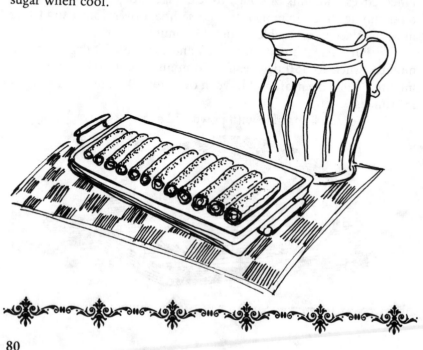

CHICKEN AND STUFFING

Make stuffing: In medium bowl, place 4 to 5 c. Italian bread, one day old, cut in cubes. Add 1 c. milk; let soak 1 hour. Mix in 1 tsp. salt, ½ tsp ground black pepper, 1 tsp. poultry seasoning, ½ c. fresh chopped parsley and 2 eggs. Mix well.

In large skillet, melt 4 Tbl. butter or margarine, add 1 (3-lb.) broiler-fryer, cut up and brown on both sides.

When chicken is browned, cover and cook over low heat for 30 minutes.

Place chicken pieces in shallow baking dish. Spread stuffing on top of chicken. Bake, uncovered, in 375 degree oven for 30 minutes or until stuffing is golden brown. Baste with ¼ c. melted butter from time to time. Makes 4 servings.

*   *   *

EGG NOODLES

Terrific in the chicken soup which appears in the Jewish section of this book.

Mix three eggs together with enough flour to make a stiff dough. Knead very well on floured board until smooth and elastic. Put under bowl for about 10 minutes to rest. Roll out on lightly floured board until very thin. Let dry for a few minutes.

Now the fun begins! Cut out circles and holes by using a doughnut cutter. To make curly noodles, cut dough into strips and wind around everything small and round in the house -- knitting needles, wooden spoon handles, etc. Let dry and pull off. Of course, you can make just plain old noodle-shaped noodles by cutting them into strips. But have fun and use cookie cutters or whatever else you want.

After the noodles have dried, package them in plastic bags or store in glass jars. They're very pretty on the kitchen counter in glass containers.

By Carole Eberly

WALNUT TORTE

10 eggs, separated   2 c. finely ground walnuts
2 c. powdered sugar

Beat egg yolks with powdered sugar. In separate bowl, beat whites until stiff but not dry. Fold whites into egg yolk mixture. Then gradually fold in walnuts. Bake in 3 greased pans at 300 degrees for 1 hours. Remove pans from oven and cool completely before removing from pans.

For filling, cream together ½ lb. butter and ½ lb. powdered sugar. Add 2 egg yolks and 1 small egg and 1 tsp. vanilla, beating well. Spread between layers, on top and sides. (If you want, sprinkle a few ground walnuts on top.) Keep in a cool place.

(You can also use whipped cream for the filling and frosting. For a chocolate filling, add some chocolate syrup to the butter cream filling.)

*　　　　　*　　　　　*

ROZKY

1½ lb. flour   1 tsp. salt
1 lb. butter   1 large can evaported milk
1 Tbl. sugar   4 egg yolks
1 Tbl. baking powder

Mix ingredients together until well. blended and dough doesn't stick to your hands. Refrigerate for 1 hour. Roll out on floured board and cut in squares. Fill with favorite filling. Roll and turn into crescents. Brush top with milk or beaten egg. Bake at 350 degrees for 30 minutes. Cool and sprinkle with powdered sugar, if desired.

*　　　　　*　　　　　*

CHEESECAKE

This is an unusual cheesecake because it doesn't have any crust -- crumb or otherwise.

2 8-oz. pkg. cream cheese	3 Tbl. cornstarch
1 lb. small curd cottage	3 Tbl. flour
cheese	1½ Tbl. lemon juice
4 eggs	1 tsp. vanilla
1½ c. sugar	1 pt. sour cream
	½ c. melted butter

Beat cream cheese, cottage cheese and sugar with eggs until well blended. Add cornstarch, flour, lemon juice and vanilla. Beat well. Add melted butter and sour cream, beating until smooth. Pour into greased 9-inch spring-form pan. Bake at 325 degrees for 1 hour and 10 minutes. Test around edges for firmness. Turn off oven and let the cake remain there for 2 hours. Remove sides of pan. Cool completely for 2 hours in refrigerator. (This cake can be frozen, and should be stored in the refrigerator.)

*   *   *

PRUNE NUT SQUARES

1 lb. ground walnuts	4 eggs
1 lb. butter	2 tsp. baking powder
1 lb. powdered sugar	1 tsp. vanilla
4 c. flour	Filling

Mix together walnuts, butter, sugar, eggs, vanilla, baking powder and flour. Roll ¾ of the dough ½-inch thick and put on greased pan. Cover with prune butter (or any other filling). Make strips of remaining dough and arrange in lattice fashion over the top. Bake at 350 degrees about 20 minutes (or until done). Cut into squares.

Nazis, Kitchen Witches and Good Food

Norwegian influence in this country was first felt in the 1800s when New York's Erie Canal opened the Great Lakes to westward expansion. Although most Scandinavian immigration was into Wisconsin, Minnesota, Iowa and the Dakotas, many halted their travels in Michigan. Drawn to the area by promises of rich land and bountiful crops, these people made the arduous trip across the Atlantic in slow sailing-ships or dirty, dangerous steam vessels. The transfer to a ship going up the Hudson came next, then to a barge across the Erie Canal, to a lake vessel bound for Detroit, and finally to a ship going up Lake Huron.

When I think today of the rigors of such a journey, it amazes me. Considering that most of these people spoke only their native tongue, it seems impossible. What was the attraction?

A geography book of 1842 describes Michigan as having two peninsulas with the Upper Peninsula "inhabited almost solely by a few Indians and but little known." The Lower Peninsula was portrayed as the "settled part" that was "level, fertile, and highly productive. Large crops of wheat, corn, oats, and barley can be obtained; while apples, pears, and other fruits grow in abundance." Unfortunately, most of the early Norwegian immigrants did not find everything quite so pleasant; and, of course, not all the immigrants went into agriculture.

By 1900, of 25,531 male Scandinavians in Michigan, 7,164 were in agriculture, 5,035 in domestic and personal service, 9,366 in manufacturing and mechanical areas, and 2,818 were miners.

The first priority of Norwegian settlers was to make money since the average family arrived here with only $50.00 in cash. So, what skills they brought with them were put to immediate use.

My grandfather came here alone with a background in agriculture and forestry. He couldn't speak English and, meaning to go

By Carl Olson

to Alpena, inadvertantly left the postal packet vessel at Harrisville, about 30 miles south.With no roads available, he walked the railroad tracks into Alpena where he found a job in one of the early lumber mills.

When he had earned enough money, he sent for his childhood sweetheart, Christina. After her arrival he continued saving his money and eventually bought an 80-acre farm near Spruce, a small Norwegian enclave to the south. There they raised five boys and a girl. The farm remains in the family and is, at this writing, owned by the last of the sons who is 87 years old.

Life on the farm was Spartan and Norwegian.The boys helped work the farm; cutting wood for the kitchen stove and for heat, plowing straight furrows with draft horses, and gathering in the bounty of nature.The girls, meanwhile, learned the arts of home and hearth.

All the young people were confirmed, in Norwegian, at the local wooden Luthern church and Norwegian was the language spoken at home.

Food was basic fare with almost all coming from the farm itself. A large root cellar in the yard, still in use, supplied vegetables throught the year. Hogs and cattle were butchered on the farm for meat. Chickens provided eggs and the seemingly never-ending chicken dinners when "everybody" stopped for Sunday dinner. Fish came from nearby Hubbard Lake.

Although Norwegian cooking relies heavily on beef, potatoes, earth vegetables, and, of course, fish, the wonderful variations and traditions are what make it so interesting. One specialty dish served during Christmas has always been lutefisk and lefse. Lutefisk is cod which has been soaked in a lye solution, then dried in the sun. When purchased, lutefisk is rock hard and could be used, perhaps, as a baseball bat. Prior to cooking, it is soaked for several days in salt water and then fresh to remove the lye. Boiled a few minutes in salted water, it is served with boiled, parsleyed potatoes and lefse.

Lefse, in turn, is a thin, unleavened potato pancake which is buttered and rolled up and usually eaten with the fingers.

Christmas is also a time for cookies and pastries that evoke fond memories in anyone fortunate enough to have been around a Norwegian kitchen that time of year. No unusual ingredients are needed, since most of the recipes are different combinations of butter, eggs, and almonds--especially the butter and eggs.

A year-round favorite of mine would have to include Norwegian meatballs with a sour cream gravy. The meat for this dish, to be really of the Norwegian variety, must be ground several times and mixed very thoroughly with the spices and other ingredients.

How did I come to be interested in Noregian settlers and cooking? Well, my father left the farm in Spruce and began working for Ford Motor Company in Detroit. He crated windshields for Model T's prior to shipping but, when his ability to speak Norwegian was discovered, he was transferred to sales, trained, and sent to Norway as the sales manager for Norway, Sweden, and Denmark. He married and I was born in Oslo.

When Nazis invaded Norway in April, 1940, my father, mother, and I escaped the war aboard the U.S. Army transport *American Legion* from Petsamo in northern Finland. The escape took us by train from Stockholm into Finland and then by bus to the port near Murmansk, Russia.

Interestingly, one of our fellow passengers was Victor Borge, the noted concert pianist and comedian. I was fortunate to meet Borge again many years later at a concert he was giving in Detroit and he remembered the voyage vividly. He spoke of mines surfacing around the ship at one point and the concern of the passengers about the vessel's safety. Needless to say, we arrived in New York safely after a ten-day, dangerous trip and my family and I went on to Alpena.

My own interest in cooking was stimulated by my marrying a marvelous cook. Watching my wife in the kitchen and discussing the various techniques was the aromatic breeze that fanned the fires of my involvement with the stove and renewed my interest in all the wonderful Norwegian dishes of my youth.

Not every recipe or experiment has worked for me the first time, but a recent gift of a Norwegian "kitchen witch" which hangs from the kitchen ceiling has undoubtedly influenced recent successes. Legend says that such a "witch" will "prevent scorching and burning of things baked on the hearth." We don't have a kitchen hearth, but my bread crusts are more golden and my soups don't burn.

SANDBAKKELS

This requires small sandbakkel pans, much like small tart pans with fluted edges. They are a special Christmas treat.

1 c. butter	½ tsp. vanilla
1 c. sugar	1 c. ground almonds
2½ c. sifted flour	Pinch of salt
2 egg yolks, 1 whole egg	

Cream butter until soft and beat in sugar, eggs and vanilla. Gradually sift in flour and add ground almonds. Work dough until well mixed. Pat into sanbakkel pans until as uniformly thin as possible. Bake at 350 degrees for 15-20 minutes or until golden brown.

*   *   *

TOMATSUPPE

This is really an old-fashioned tomato soup that really pleases.

1 can whole tomatoes	¼ tsp. baking soda
¾ can of milk, warmed	1 tsp. sugar

Heat tomatoes in separate pan to the boiling point. Add the baking soda and bring to a boil again.* Add the milk but do not return to a boil. Add the sugar and serve at once. Let your guests add their own salt and pepper.

*Too much heat at this point may cause it to curdle.

*   *   *

By Carl Olson

SPLIT PEA SOUP

In Norwegian, the word for this is ertesuppe and the way it is pronounced can enable a native to determine from what part of the country an individual comes.

1 lb. split peas	1 raw carrot, grated
3 qt. water	1 large potato, grated
1 medium onion, diced	5 slices salt pork
¼ tsp. garlic paste	¼ tsp. celery salt

Combine all ingredients and bring to a boil. Lower temperature and simmer for three hours. Remove pork slices. Serve with croutons.

*   *   *

KJOTTBOLLER

A number of Norwegians get greatly upset when these Norwegian meatballs are mistakenly attributed to another Scandinavian country. Be sure to ask the butcher to grind the beef and pork three times.

1½ lb. ground roundsteak	1 tsp. mace
½ lb. ground pork	½ tsp. ginger
2 slices of bread, broken into fine crumbs	2 Tbl. cream
	1 c. milk
2 eggs	Sour cream
¼ c. onion, finely chopped	

Mix all except the sour cream thoroughly and form into meatballs the size of a large walnut. Brown and cook until done in a heavy skillet. Use pan drippings, 2-3 Tbl. flour, and a little beef broth to make gravy. Fold in sour cream (about 1 c.) just before serving and be careful not to heat too much. High temperature may make sour cream curdle.

KRANKEKAKE

When special occasions come up, such as weddings, anniversaries, or christenings, the Norwegian cook whips up this spectacular conclusion to the festivities.

1 c. sugar	3 c. ground almonds
4 hard-cooked egg yolks, mashed	1 egg white, slightly beaten
	Granulated sugar
4 whole eggs	Almond glaze (below)
2 c. butter	Fresh strawberries or other fruit
5 c. flour	

Mix together the 1 c. sugar and egg yolks. Set aside. Beat together the whole eggs and butter. Combine the two egg mixtures. Gradually add, while kneading well, the flour and almonds.

The dough is delicate and somewhat difficult to handle. Lightly flour your hands and roll a small lump on a pastry cloth into a ½ inch thick strip which is long enough to form a circle eight or nine inches in diameter. This is for the bottom ring of the pyramid. It is best to roll out all the strips first, making each one a little shorter than the last. To join the ends of the strips of dough, dip them in the egg white.

Place the rings on several slightly floured cookie sheets. You can manage three or more rings to a sheet. Sprinkle with sugar. Bake at 350 degrees about 7 minutes or until light brown. When removed from the oven, immediately place one ring on top of the other so they will adhere to each other. When cooled, drizzle with Almond Glaze and decorate with fruit.

Almond Glaze: Mix or blend 1¼ c. confectioners' sugar with ¼ c. milk. Add ½ tsp. vanilla, ¼ tsp. of butter flavoring and ¼ tsp. almond extract. Mix well.

*   *   *

On Indian Medicine --
Including Love Potions

He was mostly Ottawa, with maybe a trace of Canadian French -- a big, rangy, soft-spoken man with skin the color of old saddle-leather. Nobody knew his real age. Joe himself admitted to sixty, but there were men at the Indian village, themselves in their sixties, who said they remembered Joe as a grown man when they were just boys.

Whatever his age, Joe was a good man on the farm, and he knew more about wildlife and wood-lore than any man I ever met. And he was the prettiest thing with an axe that you ever saw. In using an axe, the idea is to let the axe do the work, and Joe was a living illustration of that principle: without even breathing hard Joe could chop through an eight-inch green maple log faster than two ordinary men with a cross-cut saw. I used to fancy myself as an axe-man, but after seeing Joe work I had to admit I was strictly bush-league.

Joe was an orphan, He lost both parents at an early age in a 'flu epidemic and was brought up by relatives who lived near Muskegon. Uncle John Joe and Auntie Florence (as Joe always called them) were Potawatomies, and I wondered about that because I'd read somewhere that the Ottawas and Potawatomies were enemies. But Joe explained that that wasn't exactly so. They were enemies of a sort and used to have a scrap once in a while just for the hell of it, but they didn't hate each other as some peoples do, and there was even some intermarriage. Most Michigan Indians were peaceable folk. They were a different breed of cat from, say, the Oglala Sioux who creamed old Yellor Hair at the Little Big Horn.

"That Custer wasn't very smart," Joe, who had done some reading on the subject, remarked one day. "If he'd listened to Bloody Knife, he'd of been all right."

By Lawrence Wakefield

"Who was Bloody Knife?"

"He was one of Custer's scouts. A Crow Indian."

"A fink, then," I said. But Joe didn't know the word.

Secretly he was proud, I think, that for once the Indians had got a little of their own back, but he was too polite to say so. I told him I didn't think much of Custer either.

Mrs. Louisa Wiggins took an active part in the wild rice harvest of Michigan Indians. Here she is shown scorching the rice in 1958 when she was 84 years old. *(Photo from Michigan State Archives)*

Uncle John Joe was chief of the Muskegon band, and Auntie Florence was the medicine-woman. She used to take Joe along on foraging trips in the woods to hunt for the herbs and roots and berries that she used in making her medicine.

"Did you ever wonder why Indians don't get cancer?" Joe asked me one day.

"I didn't know they didn't," I said. "But then, I don't know many Indians."

"They don't get it," Joe said. "They got a medicine for it."

"Maybe they ought to share it with the rest of the world," I suggested.

"Wouldn't do any good," Joe said gloomily. "They'd just call it superstition. And it doesn't work if you don't believe in it."

Joe was as smart as businessmen or bankers, and he was very serious about Indian medicine; he really believed in it. He told me that the Indians had a cure for almost everything except some of the white man's diseases, and I got the impression that, in the olden time, Indians never died of anything except old age or an accident -- until the white man introduced him to firearms, firewater and 'flu.

In the long summer evenings Joe and I would sometimes go out in the woods, and he would point out some of the plants that he and Auntie Florence had collected for medicine. Some of those that I recognized were goldenrod, clubmoss, wormwood, Seneca grass, chickory and savory.

Auntie Florence also made love potions. There were two kinds of love potions, Joe said. One was made of the feet of a toad. You dried the feet over a slow fire, and then ground them into a fine powder. Then you dropped a pinch of it in your girl's coffee or tea when she wasn't looking. It was pretty good medicine, Joe said, but it didn't always work. The tree-toad, Joe explained, is a capricious fellow and sometimes he's willing and sometimes he isn't. If he isn't willing, the medicine doesn't work.

The other kind of love potion, though, is sure-fire. You make it with leeches (those wormy little fellows that swim around in stagnat shallow water, Joe said). The leeches are dried and powdered in the same way. And if you slip a pinch of *this* medicine in a girl's tea, she will follow you for the rest of her life. But it was a dangerous medicine, Joe said; it was nothing to fool around with. Only rarely, and for what she considered a compelling reason, could Auntie Florence be persuaded to make it.

Joe gave me lessons in the Ottawa language as we worked together on the farm. One of the first things that I learned was there are no swear-words in Ottawa. You can't cuss out a man or question his parentage in the Indian language nor can you take the name of the Lord in vain. This is just another advantage that civilized people had over the Indian, to whom profanity and obscenity were unknown concepts.

Joe was a good man and a good friend. He has long ago gone to the Happy Hunting Ground, and I hope he found everything he wanted there, I may see him again some time, and we will talk some Indian if I can still remember the words.

I'd like to meet Uncle John Joe and Auntie Flo, too. I'm still curious about that love medicine. I had a notion to try it once -- the potent kind, the one with the bloodsuckers -- but I chickened out. As Joe said, it isn't something you want to fool around with. And what would I do, a happily married man, if it really works?

BRUNSWICK STEW

3 slices bacon	2 potatoes, cut up
4-5 lb. frying chicken, cut up	1 stalk celery
2 c. corn	2 tsp. salt
2 c. lima beans	¼ tsp. pepper
3 tomatoes	2 c. chicken stock

Cut bacon in small pieces and fry. Remove bacon and brown chicken pieces in fat. Place chicken, fat and other ingredients with bacon in ovenproof casserole. Cover and cook 1 hour at 325 degrees. Serve with corn pone.

*   *   *

CORN PONE

Mix 2 c. conrmeal, 1 tsp. salt and piece of lard the size of an egg. Pour in enough boiling water to moisten sufficiently to press into molds. Pack into molds, baking in 350 degree oven about 30 minutes. They should be crusty on the outside, soft on the inside.

*   *   *

PUMPKIN SOUP

(1 lb. 13 oz.) can pumpkin	¼ tsp. cinnamon
4 c. milk	¼ tsp. mace
2 Tbl. butter	¼ tsp. ground cloves
2 Tbl. honey	1 tsp. salt
3 Tbl. brown sugar	Juice of 1 orange

Heat together pumpkin, milk, butter and honey. Stir in brown sugar and spices. Add orange juice, a little at a time, stirring constantly. Do not boil. Serve hot.

INDIAN BREAD

3 c. flour
1¾ c. corn meal
1 tsp. baking soda
1½ tsp. salt

½ tsp. nutmeg
3½ c. milk
1 c. molasses

Mix together dry ingredients. Combine milk and molasses; pour into dry ingredients, beating until smooth. Pour into 2-qt. steam mold. Cover and place on rack in deep kettle with tight-fitting lid. Put in enough boiling water to come about half-way up the mold. Cover and steam about 3 hours. Remove mold from kettle and let stand 20 minutes. Remove mold cover and let stand another 10 minutes. Loosen edges of pudding with spatula, invert on a plate and let stand until pudding unmolds. Serve with butter.

*　　　　　*　　　　　*

CORN CHOWDER

2 c. corn
2 Tbl. butter
1 small onion

1 Tbl. flour
3 c. evaporated milk
Salt and pepper

Cook corn and onion in butter until tender. Stir in the flour. Slowly add milk, stirring until thick. Season with salt and pepper.

*　　　　　*　　　　　*

BAKED ACORN SQUASH

2 acorn squashes
4 Tbl. butter
4 tsp. maple sugar or
　brown sugar

4 Tbl. honey
Salt and pepper
Nutmeg

Bake whole squashes in a 325 degree oven for about 1 hour. Remove from oven, cut in half and scoop out pulp and seeds. Dot each with ¼ of the butter, honey, sugar and spices. Bake at 325 degrees about 1½ hours, or until tender.

INDIAN PUDDING

3 c. hot milk	1 tsp. salt
1½ c. raisins	½ c. sugar
1½ c. cold milk	¾ tsp. ginger
1 c. corn meal	¼ tsp. nutmeg
½ c. molasses	¼ c. butter
2 Tbl. maple or brown sugar	

Soak raisins in hot milk. Mix 1 c. cold milk with the corn meal. Stir into raisin mixture. Heat slowly, stirring constantly for about 15 minutes, or until mixture thickens. Mix in molasses, salt, sugar, ginger, nutmeg and butter. Pour into a greased 2-qt. casserole. Pour remaining ½ c. milk into the center of pudding. Set casserole in pan of cold water and bake at 300 degrees for 2½ hours. Let cool for 3-4 hours before serving. Serve with sweetened whipped cream.

*   *   *

VENISON AND WILD RICE

4 lb. shoulder of venison, cut into 2-inch cubes	2 tsp. salt
8 c. water	¼ tsp. pepper
3 onions, peeled and quartered	1½ c. wild rice

Simmer venison, water and onions uncovered for 3 hours, or until tender. Mix in remaining ingredients. Cover and simmer for 20 minutes. Stir. Simmer uncovered about 20 more minutes, or until most of the liquid is absorbed.

*   *   *

The Legman with Sore Feet

In the days of vaudeville, the comics used to have a gag line that went something like this, "What do two Greeks do when they get together? They start a restaurant."

The fast-patter actors weren't kidding. About ninety per cent of the eating establishments in the United States from the turn of the century until the 1950s were operated by Greeks who came from the old country.

Having a firsthand observation of both professions -- acting and restauranting – at close view and from personal experience it seems that in those alleged good old days the Greek restaurants provided as many laughs as performers.

Many gag lines dealing with Greek accents became part of the routine lifted from dialogues overheard by actors in so-called "greasy spoon" eating establishments that were near their theaters where they performed three or four times a day in vaudeville routines for small pay in the struggle for histrionic fame.

The way I got into the act – both in the restaurant and theater field -- was because of geographical proximity. I worked next door to an RKO movie theater in the days when attending a vaudeville show or a film showing was considered the highlight of entertainment, along with church ice cream socials.

There is an old wheeze to the effect one is not in a position to pick his own parents or relatives. Some of my favorite people are Greeks, including my father and mother and their parents who came from Sparta and the Hellenic hills, plus many nice kin folk.

Jim, my father, and Uncle Charles Zarafonetis settled in Hillsboro, Texas and had an ornate confectionary store featuring marbled, mirrored showcases with numerous candies, cigars and

By George Zarafonetis

97

cigarettes. The soda fountain offered sodas, malted milks, milk shakes, grape juice, Dr. Pepper and Coca Cola. The store made a "killing" because just before 1900 Hillsboro -- a county seat -- voted down beer and liquor on account of such characters as John Wesley Hardin and other big name fighters kept frequenting the saloons in the area for the inevitable shootouts like in fiction and the movies.

When Dad died in 1925 at the age of 49, my mother, Helen, and I moved with my three kid brothers to Grand Rapids where she had a brother, Tom Skouros. Tom owned a soda bar and restaurant next to the Keith Theater.

That was when Jack Benny, Ed Wynne and Eddie Cantor, among others, were on enforced diets because of economics when they played the vaudeville house in Grand Rapids. Down a nearby alley was the old Powers Theater where Spencer Tracy and other well-known players performed on their circuits before they became famous.

I was 16 at the time when I was permitted a view of the stars of tomorrow. The opportunity was afforded because I delivered sandwiches and cokes to the performers and showgirls in the lineups -- fifty feet from our kitchen. It enabled me to get acquainted with the names who later became big on the marquees, and their bank accounts and ribs fattened.

It also enabled me to work my way through high school. Before I clutched the diploma, I had worked in thirty-seven local restaurants in Grand Rapids. It was nice work but we toiled twelve hours a day and night which handicapped both sleep and school work. The reason for "floating" on jobs was to get a night off once in a while.

When the big stock market crash came in 1929, eating became a problem. It got so bad that one restaurant served fifteen-cent meals in Grand Rapids (small doses, that is).

Finally, I told my mother as long as I couldn't make any money I wanted to travel and see parts of the United States, all of which seemed to be disturbed economically. My first stop was Baltimore where a cousin, George Zarafonetis, also named, had several concessions in the Bellaire Market. Because of our close relationship, I was assigned to the peanut stand. The four-block square market had a top but was open at the sides which did nothing to protect the wind from blowing in during the winter months, which I unfortunately chose for my visit.

It was rewarding. I not only had fun but gave Ted Lewis, the great actor and musician, a big boost on his appearance at the Valencia Theater. Lewis featured "When My Baby Smiles at Me," "Me and My Shadow" and "The Peanut Vendor Song." When Lewis started his peanut song, he tossed peanuts into the audience. That's when I and several of my friends got into the act and showered down four bags of peanuts to the stage and front seats from our balcony seats. The peanuts weren' t selling anyway.

From Baltimore it was on to Pittsburgh and Sophie's restaurant in East Liberty. It was just another stop. Sophie's was so hard up for business it put up a sign, "All You Can Eat For Fifty Cents." I couldn't take it too long. The day a guy who had been saving up for two weeks came in for a gastronomic orgy and ordered his third meat and sixth salad serving plus repeated coffee refills, I took off my apron and headed for other hills.

This time I went to South Bend, Indiana where I worked at the famous Philadelphia Cafe, operated by Eustace Poledor and his brothers, Pendell and Andy. It was a hangout for Notre Dame students and an outstanding confectionery and restaurant.

The schedule called for three months in each city and included jobs in Boston at the old Alpha lunch chain and several trips back and forth to Texas. I then discarded the apron and went to work in the newspaper business where I became known as the "Legman with Sore Feet." But I lasted forty-five years and three months and two days before retiring to snow covered pastures in Michigan.

BEEF WITH ONIONS
(Stifatho Stew)

2 lb. boneless chuck beef	½ c. vinegar
½ c. olive oil	1 small can tomatoes
4 lb. small onions	5 cloves garlic
1 tsp. whole pickling spice	Salt and pepper to taste

Cut meat in small pieces; brown slightly in oil. Peel onions and leave whole. Add to meat, together with spices (in a metal tea ball or tied in clean cheesecloth), vinegar, tomatoes, garlic and seasoning. Add a little water, cover tightly and cook until meat and onions are tender and liquid is reduced to a delicious gravy. Remove spices at once.

Lamb or rabbit meat stews follow same recipe.

*   *   *

GREEK SALAD

The traditional Greek salad for many generations has consisted of a vegetable or greens boiled in salted water and eaten cold with the addition of oil, vinegar, or lemon juice, salt and a little pepper. Greens and vegetables prepared and served in this manner are numerous, some of which are:

Dandelion greens	Cauliflower
Beet tops and beets	Swiss chard
Cabbage	Asparagus
Spinach	Endive
Squash	Escarolle

Variations of Greek salads include the addition of tomatoes, onions, Feta cheese, sardines and garlic.

STUFFED GRAPE LEAVES
(Dolmathes)

50 grape leaves, fresh or canned	½ c. rice
1 large onion	½ c. chopped parsley and mint
1 lb. ground steak	2 tsp. salt
3 Tbl. butter	Pepper to taste

Wash fresh leaves thoroughly. If canned leaves are used scald first in hot water to remove excess brine.

Filling: Fry chopped onion in melted butter until golden. Then mix with meat, rice and seasonings.

Take one teaspoon of filling and place in center of one large leaf or two small ones, being sure that shiny side of leaf is underneath, or on outside, when rolled. Carefully fold over top and sides like an envelope and roll up like miniature football. Place a few coarse leaves in bottom of pot. Carefully arrange the balls on top, side by side and in layers until all filling and leaves are used. Add two cups of water and a little butter and salt. Place a heavy plate on top and simmer for a ½ hour or longer if needed. Serve hot with egg and lemon sauce made from 3 eggs beaten slightly with lemon juice and 5-6 tsp. liquid from the leaves.

*   *   *

BAKED MEATBALLS
(Keftethes Psimenes)

1 lb. ground beef	½ tsp. pepper
1½ lb. ground pork	½ tsp. cinnamon
1 egg	1 tsp. olive oil
3 slices dry bread	1/3 tsp. baking soda dissolved in 1 c. red wine
1 onion, chopped fine	
1 tsp. peppermint leaves	1 tsp. tomato puree
1 tsp. salt	

Mix all ingredients well and shape into round patties. Place on a greased cookie sheet and bake till done. Serve plain or with a tomato sauce.

HONEY CURLS
(Theples)

4 eggs	¼ c. butter
2½ c. flour	Honey
½ tsp. baking powder	Cinnamon
½ tsp. salt	Chopped walnuts (optional)

Beat eggs until very light and beat in 2 c. flour, baking powder and salt. Work in other ½ c. of flour and a little more if necessary to make a soft dough that does not stick to the fingers. Turn dough onto a board and spread lightly with butter. Work in butter with hands, a little at a time. Knead dough until it is smooth and soft. Cut dough in four parts. Roll one part on floured board until paper thin, keep remainder of dough covered until use to avoid drying. Use a pastry wheel to cut into 4x6 inch pieces.

Drop into hot olive oil or shortening, at 365 degrees. Using two forks, turn dough over immediately and roll quickly, like a jelly roll, before it becomes crisp. Fry until very lightly browned. Drain on absorbent paper. Dilute honey with a little hot water and dribble over the curls. Sprinkle with cinnamon and finely chopped nuts. Theples are best eaten with fingers as they break if pierced with a fork.

DIAMOND PASTRY DELIGHT
(Easy Baklava)

2 lb. chopped walnuts	1½ lb. butter
2 tsp. cinnamon	2 lb. pastry sheets
1 tsp. cloves	

Combine walnuts and spices in large mixing bowl. Melt butter and brush bottom of a 14x20 inch pan with it. Place one pastry sheet in the pan. Brush with melted butter and repeat process until four pastry sheets line the bottom of the baking pan. Brush fourth layer with melted butter and sprinkle with nut mixture. Repeat the process until all the ingredients are used, ending with four top layers. Brush top with butter and cut into diamond shapes. A clove bud may be placed in center of each Diamond Pastry Delight, if desired. Bake for 1 hour at 300 degrees until golden brown. While pastry is baking prepare syrup.

Syrup:

1 pt. honey	2 lb. sugar
½ tsp. lemon flavor	Juice of 1 lemon

Boil syrup ingredients together. Cool and using a spoon pour slowly over the baklava.

"Use the Shotgun on Him"

It took great courage for those European immigrants to leave the stable life in the "Old Country" and quit their native shores for the promise of a better life in the wilderness of Northern Michigan, there to hew out their homesteads in an almost pathless forest. It was still a land of Indians and a few venturesome settlers. No roads traversed the regions when they first came. Pine, hemlock and maples stood dark and thick to block their coming. Bear, wolves and other wildlife were numerous. What neighbors had preceded them were often miles away and all communication was over Indian moccasin trails, dimly discernible in the deep woods.

August Krans, his wife and two children left the rugged shores of their native Sweden to seek a home in this new land beyond the Great Lakes. Krans had the promise of work in the recently opened iron ore mine at Vulcan in the Upper Peninsula of Michigan. Here he found wages low and seasonal layoffs frequent. Life there was harder than they had been led to expect.

One day Krans heard of the new government lands which had just been opened to homesteaders up north. On a May morning of 1881 he gathered his three mining partners in his little rented home and told them of the great opportunity awaiting men of courage and industry in the land beyond. There were Charles Gustafson, Gottfried Norden and Ole Benson, each of whom had preceded Krans out of Sweden and had each experienced disappointment with their small incomes at the Vulcan mine.

Pooling their meager cash resources, the four men engaged a goverment surveyor, packed a few provisions and a blanket each, bid goodbye to their wives and children and set off on foot to explore the possibities in that new promised land.

They covered the thirty-five miles from Vulcan to Chicaugon

By Lewis C. Reimann   (*Mr. Reimann, now deceased, was a native of Iron River. He wrote colorful, witty tales of the old U.P. -- complete with accounts of saints, sinners and strange folks.*)   *Reprinted with permission from "Between the Iron and the Pine" by Lewis C. Reimann, copyright 1951 by Lewis C. Reimann.*

Lake in Bates Township, then still a part of Marquette County. Here on the pine and birch-covered shore they made camp the second afternoon. Krans acted as cook and walked down to the lake for a pail of water to brew tea. As he dipped his bucket in the water his eyes fell on an old Indian birchbark canoe tied to a tree. Being of an inquisitive nature, he approached it and saw that it was covered by a ragged woolen blanket. He raised the blanket to find the body of a dead white man lying on the bottom of the craft. He ran back to the camping spot and reported his find to the other three. Not knowing the meaning of Krans' upsetting discovery, they held a brief council. Fearing what their own fate might be in this unknown Indian Country, they decided to move on. They picked up their packs and hiked hurriedly west to Stambaugh, a settlement of a few log houses, where they felt safe again.

A few days later, after being assured by the Stambaugh people that the Indians in that territory were friendly and harmless, unless they were under the influence of firewater, the four men walked back to Bates Township and with the assistance of the surveyor staked out a section of 640 acres of timber land, each taking 160 acres to clear and build a house upon. This was Section 23, later to become known as Little Sweden.

In order to prevent anyone else "jumping" their claim, the homesteaders decided to stay a month to make a small clearing and erect a log cabin, They located a spring in the middle of the section and cut trails from it to their own cabins. Then together they trekked back to Vulcan, gathered their families, packed their belongings and walked all the way back to their new homes. Krans carried a small cookstove on his back the thiry-five miles, assisted by his wife and two children who had heavy packs of their own. Here they hacked out the pine and hardwoods to make a small clearing between the stumps. Edible game, deer, partridge, bear and fish were abundant, and close at hand for the shooting or angling. Their lives were hard and their work endless, but they made progress and their hopes were ever high.

An outcropping of iron ore was discovered in the neighborhood and explorers began to stake out new claims. One day while Krans was on a trip to Stambaugh for supplies, a man named Boardman came to his home and ordered Mrs. Krans off the land, stating that it was his claim. The woman comprehended little English but got the gist of his remarks. Unfamiliar with the land laws, Krans made three trips to the Land Office at Lansing to protect his rights. Each time the land agent assured him that his claim was valid. On the third visit the agent asked him:

"How far is your house from the property line?"

"About 500 yards," replied Krans.

"Then, here, take this shotgun with you and when Boardman comes again, give him five minutes to get off your property. If he isn't off by that time, use the shotgun on him."

The next time Boardman appeared, Krans was home. He gave the claim-jumper five minutes to get to the property line. Telling about it later, Krans said:

"By yimminy, dat feller made it in t'ree."

Within two years Krans bought a horse which he used on the farm and to haul stovewood into town in the winter time The four homesteaders each bought a cow and walked them over the Indian trail from Stambaugh to their farms. When one cow went dry, the other animals supplied the milk for the four families.

In the meantime iron ore was discovered in the Iron River district and the Isabella mine was the first to dig and ship ore to the docks at Escanaba over the newly extended Chicago & Northwestern Railroad. Krans secured work at the new mine at a wage of one dollar a day for a twelve-hour day, six days a week. He walked the distance of ten miles to the mine and ten miles back each day. In his "spare time" he cleared the land, planted his crops, harvested, cut wood and logs to sell to the mills. Deer ate their crops , for no fence could be built high enough to keep them out. Although their chief source of meat supply was venison, they could not shoot enough deer to protect their vegetables and grain. Bear broke into their pig-pen and carried off their youg pigs. The young stock had to be kept close to the clearing during the day and locked up in the barn at night to prevent them from falling victims of bear and wolves.

The greatest hardship was borne by Mrs. Krans. She arose at four in the morning to prepare her husband's breakfast and pack his pail before he set off, while it was still dark, for his work at the mine. The family gradually grew from the original two who had walked in from Vulcan to a total of thirteen—seven boys and six girls. Their mother was never attended by a doctor at child-birth and was up and at work within two or three days after the new arrival, tending her household duties and caring for the rest of her brood. Krans had a doctor only once in his life in the wilderness, when he had an attack of pneumonia and was attended by Dr. Fred Bond, the husband of Carrie Jacobs Bond.

Mrs. Krans, in addition to caring for her children and working in the fields and kitchen, found it necessary to carry water from the spring a quarter of a mile down the hill. Not trusting the wandering bands of Indians, and fearing the more savage packs of timber wolves which ranged the forests, she carried one or two younger children to and from the spring while weighted down by a shoulder-yoke loaded with heavy pails of water.

As though life in the wilderness was not hard enough and six days of work at the mines at $1.00 a day for twelve hours a day not discouraging enough to this courageous family, the depression of 1893 added even greater burdens. The mines closed and families were thrown almost completely on the land. Shouldering the rifles, the men brought in deer, rabbits and occasionally a bear to feed the hungry mouths in the little log cabins in Bates township. Krans and his neighbors found occasional work cutting four-foot hardwood at sixty-five cents a cord for the charcoal kilns near the Mansville Waite farm, earning from fifty to seventy-five cents a day, which began before daylight and ended after dark. The struggle to keep the bread-box filled was bitter and long. Families living on homesteads were

Women Pose for the Swedish Festival in Cadillac. Year.....? *(Photo from Michigan State Photo Archives)*

more fortunate than those living in town, for they were sure of at least potato soup with a bit of venison or saltpork.

As the children grew, each one had his specific duties on the farm, even while attending the little log school. The boys helped their father with the farm work, cutting wood, caring for the stock and clearing the land. The girls assisted their mother in the house and with cooking, washing, ironing, and scrubbing. When that work was done, they worked in the fields with the men. The most prosperous time the family enjoyed in the early days was one winter when they cut, sawed and split and sold to people in town a total of three hundred cords of stovewood.

Mr. and Mrs. Krans knew just how long it should take the children to return from school in the afternoon and outlined in advance the field or house work each must accomplish, according to their size, sex and strength, and woe to any slacker on the assignment!

As new neighbors took up claims and homesteads, life became easier. Roads were built and a Swedish Lutheran Church was erected. Practically all the inhabitants in Bates were Swedish immigrants. The Swedish language was practically the only language spoken except in school and in town. Most children had never heard a word of English until they entered the first grade. Anyone not a Swede in the township was considered a "foreigner", even though his parents were native Americans. Non-Swedes could not find employment on any of the farms or the woods owned by the Swedes. First generation Americans in this community spoke with a decided Swedish accent their entire lives.

Despite their hardships, or perhaps because of them, eleven of the Krans children survived, all were married and all but one continued to live in the Iron River district. Over forty grand-children attested to the ruggedness of this hardy pioneer stock which migrated from Sweden to join their neighbors in building a little Sweden in the wilds of this unknown country, and to carve out a home, a living and an enviable reputation with their bare hands.

SMORGASBOARD ETIQUETTE

There is a correct way to eat a smorgasbord instead of just diving in and piling your plate two-feet high. First, start with the herring (pickled, marinated, in sour cream, smoked, fried, etc.) and anchovy dishes. The next step is to take a clean plate and wade through the fish dishes (smoked salmon and eel, bass with horseradish, etc.). Now comes the liver paste, cold cuts and salads (baked ham, liver loaf, smoked thuringer, pickled cucumbers, pickled beets, potato salad, fish and gelatin salads). Still hungry? Head into the warm dishes such as meat balls, kidneys, herring au gratin, mushroom omelet and stuffed shoulder of veal. Next follows dessert, usually a piece of cheese on hardtack or a fruit salad. The last course is served in your kitchen -- a teaspoon of baking soda mixed in a glass of water.

PICKLED HERRING*

1 c. sugar	2 pepper corns
½ c. cider vinegar	Dash red pepper
½ c. water	Herring (skinned, boned,
6 cloves	washed and drained)
2 bay leaves	Onion slices

Boil all but herring and onion slices for 3 minutes. Pour over herring and onion. Refrigerate 6-7 hours.

*   *   *

GLOGG*

Cover 1½ lb. raisins with water in a pan. Add 1½ c. sugar, 1 Tbl. broken cinnamon sticks and 1 Tbl. whole cloves. Crack 24 cardamon seeds and put shells and all in pan. Stir and cover. Simmer 2 hours. Add more water, if necessary.

Remove from heat. Add 1 gallon red burgundy wine and bring almost to a simmer. Keep hot and 2 hours. Then cool. Let set overnight. Next day, drain out the spices. Squeeze out the raisins. Pour into a bottle for storage. When ready to serve, reheat and add a fifth of brandy.

*   *   *

PICKLED BEETS

2 large cans sliced beets	5-6 whole cloves
¾ c. sugar	Salt and pepper
1½ c. vinegar	

Heat sugar, vinegar and spices. Pour over beets and let stand, refrigerated, 6-7 hours before serving.

---

*By GAY EBERLY

PICKLED CUCUMBERS

2-3 cucumbers
1 c. sugar
1½ c. vinegar

Salt and pepper
2 Tbl. chopped parsley

Peel cucumbers and groove them with a fork. Slice thin. Heat sugar, vinegar, salt and pepper. Pour over cucumbers and chill 2-3 hours. Sprinkle with parsley.

*   *   *

RYE BREAD

1 c. milk
1 pkg. yeast
2 Tbl. sugar
1 c. very warm water
4½ c. unbleached flour
¾ c. dark corn syrup
1 tsp. fennel seeds

1 tsp. aniseed
1/3 c. butter
Grated rind of 1 orange
1½ tsp. salt
3 c. rye flour
Lukewarm water

Scald milk and cool to lukewarm. Sprinkle yeast and sugar into water in large bowl. Let stand until dissolved. Stir in milk. Beat in 3 c. unbleached flour. Cover and let rise until doubled, 1-1½ hours. Heat syrup, fennel and aniseed in saucepan until boiling. Cool to lukewarm. Beat syrup, butter, orange rind and salt into risen batter. Stir in rye flour and 1 c. unbleached flour. Use remaining flour for kneading. Knead until smooth and elastic, about 10-15 minutes. Place in greased bowl, turning to grease all sides. Cover and let rise until doubled, about 1-2 hours.

Shape into 2 loaves. Grease 2 bread pans and place inside. Cover and let rise until doubled, about 1 hour. Bake at 375 degrees for 35 minutes. Brush with lukewarm water and bake 5 minutes longer.

SWEDISH OVEN PANCAKE

4 eggs	¾ tsp. salt
2 c. milk	4 Tbl. butter
1 c. flour	

Beat together eggs, milk, flour and salt. Melt butter in 9x13 baking dish. Pour ingredients into dish and bake at 425 degrees for 25 minutes, or until set. Cut into squares and serve with lingonberries, syrup or jam.

*　　　　　*　　　　　*

THUMBPRINT COOKIES

¾ c. sugar	½ tsp. almond extract
1 tsp. salt	2 c. flour
¾ c. butter	2 egg whites
2 egg yolks	1½ c. chopped walnuts
½ tsp. vanilla	½ c. jam or jelly

Beat together sugar, salt, butter, yolks, vanilla and almond extract. Blend in flour until well mixed. Roll dough into 1-inch balls. Dip balls into slightly beaten egg whites, then roll in nuts. Place on greased cookie sheets. Make a depression in center of each cookie with thimble or finger. Bake at 350 degrees for 10-12 minutes. While warm, fill center with jam or jelly. (You may have to re-thimble the cookies in the oven about halfway through the baking period.

*　　　　　*　　　　　*

Two Remarkable Escapees, Liars

Felek and Teklunia are their names. They were runaways, escapees, liars. Most Poles who came to America around 1910-1912, especially those from Polish Russia and Polish Germany, had to lie, because restrictions on travel (and life) were severe. So they lied about their ages, their reasons for crossing a border, their very names.

Felek was 19, the age of Russian conscription, and had been detained six months for questioning as a suspected member of a Polish underground organization (Polska Partia Socjalistyczna). He was not a member and was released but his friends and family feared for his safety. So he obtained a pass to Austrian Poland on the pretext of visiting an aunt. From there, he left for America.

Teklunia was 16, the oldest of six children. Her widowed mother needed help with work on the land and in the house. The solution was a simple, common one: marry Teklunia off and get a man, a strong worker, into the home. An aunt in the next village knew of a man who was willing and made the arrangements. Teklunia rebelled. The thought of marrying a stranger was completely repugnant. So one morning she started off, presumably to her daily chore of milking the cow, left the milk cans behind the stable door, and walked out of the village to meet some friends who were leaving for America.

Both Felek and Teklunia agree that the seven-day passage across the ocean was pleasant enough. The food was good--for those who were able to keep it down. They were treated well. Coming from abject poverty, they did not expect royal suites on board ship and weren't particularly aware of overcrowding or inconvenience.

By Regina Koscielski

Reprinted with permission from "Immigrants and Migrants: The Detroit Ethnic Experience", copright by Wayne State University Studies and Weekend College. Originally titled "Portrait of a Polish-American."

113

One landed in New York, the other in Montreal. Both cities had similar procedures for the immigrants. There were translators, there were prople who put them on the right trains to the right destinations. Felek did not like the identification tag which all had pinned on their clothes, so he tore his off and threw it out. This caused some difficulties, such as having to take a taxi and being overcharged.

Then began the new life in America: living in boarding houses, looking for work, working harder than they ever had to in Europe, making foolish mistakes, being insulted ("Polander" was the prevalent term of derision). Being misunderstood because of the language barrier, sometimes being laughed at, more often being helped. Eventually, both came to Detroit, met and married.

Owning a home in a "Polish" neighborhood was of prime importance. Saving enough for a down payment and then meeting the monthly payment was always the first thing taken care of from the meagre pay check. They shared the heavy work around that house. When a load of coal was delivered, Teklunia shoveled it into a wheelbarrow and into the coal bin. It was cheaper that way; she saved the 25-cent-a-ton wheeling-in charge. She helped lay sidewalks and put up fences. Many a bitter neighborhood feud was started over boundaries, so their fences were installed very carefully; not an inch was taken from or given to the neighbors.

There had to be a garden with carrots, parsley, onions, beets, and tomatoes, to be eaten in season and canned and stored for the winter. There had to be a lawn, neatly trimmed and weeded. There had to be flowers—many different varieties for continuous bloom and for trading with the neighbors. Seeds were gathered and stored for the next spring—one could not afford to buy flower seeds every year! During the spring and summer, to keep these vegetables, flowers and lawn thriving, there was the daily ritual of watering, even on the days it rained. There had to be a downpour to warrant skipping a day, to consider that God had done a good job of sprinkling that day!

Felek had learned a trade in Poland, tile stove-fitting ("kaflarstwo"), which was completely useless in America. So he did factory work. Those were pre-union days, when working conditions were truly difficult. Frequently he complained about his foreman and company policies, but he was proud of his contribution to the auto industry. When he saw a Cadillac on the road, he would say: "There! My work is on that Cadillac. Every fender of every Cadillac is welded by me. I do a good job!" This simple, untrained man did all his own work around the house: electrical, plumbing, painting, carpentry. He cut his children's hair and repaired their shoes. When you cannot afford to hire someone, you learn to do it yourself -- somehow.

Teklunia, too, was proud of herself as a worker. Before her marriage, when she was hired as a dishwasher in a restaurant, she burned her hands because she made the water too hot. She was so determined that those dishes should be really clean. During the Depression, when the going got tough, she worked in a hotel, washing floors, windows, toilets. Many a fine lady requested that she be her permanent cleaning woman.

This Polish-American couple was never too proud to do any kind of work. All honest work was important. They were too proud only to ask for help—to "go on welfare." Asking for help from the Welfare Department was the final, most desperate step a family took. Felek and Teklunia worked, scrimped and denied themselves to avoid such a calamity. They succeeded.

America was a good place. They were making progress while their families in Poland were standing still. There was homesickness for loved ones, but there was no yearning to return to their living conditions. America was their country now. To become an American citizen, Felek went to night school to learn English. By that time they had children, and it was their 10-year-old daughter who had the task of drilling her father on the possible questions the judge might ask: The Constitution, the three branches of Government, who was the first President, who was the present Governor. He studied, he worried, he passed the test ... he received those precious citizenship papers.

Teklunia did not think papers were that important. She was here, she felt American. Until World War II. Then she had to register as an alien. What an insult! "I have two sons in the Army and they say I'm not an American?" She registered as an alien one day and applied for citizenship the next day. But she did not pore over any books. Felek worried, "You won't pass. Your're not studying about the Constitution!" "Don't fret, I read the newspapers; I listen to the radio; I know what's going on. And I have two sons in the Army!" She made it -- with flying colors! -- red, white and blue!

These colors are respected deeply. No national holiday goes by without Felek hanging out the American flag on the front porch. The neighbors have a friendly contest going: who will be the first to display the flag on the morning of a holiday? Shame on the one who forgets to bring it in by dusk!

American citizens, they both vote. Every election without fail. And, of course, they vote "straight Democratic." No newspaper editor, no radio commentator can change that. After all, President Wilson was a Democrat and he put Poland back on the map with his Fourteenth Point after World War I. So Roosevelt sold Poland down the river at Yalta? He must have been sick or got some bad advice. But Roosevelt saved our home (through the HOLC) when we almost lost it during the Depression, and Roosevelt was for the working man. Democrats are always for the working man; Republicans are for the rich people.

The Church was important to them -- to a point. They believed that no church ever taught anyone to do bad things so all churches were good. However, since they were born and raised as Catholics, they went to the Catholic Church. They felt that not all priests were good – many of them just wanted their hands kissed and their palms crossed with silver. But there were those priests "z powolania" (with a true vocation), who were admired and supported. The nuns, on the other hand, were ALL dedicated, holy women. As teachers they were unsurpassed. Felek and Teklunia -- along with their contemporaries -- truly believed that Polish parochial schools, taught by these good nuns, gave children a far better education than public schools could. What other proof was needed than the fact that these parochial schools taught their children Polish and catechism as well as English? So it was the Catholic schools which were their principal concern, rather than the Catholic churches.

Education was important. They appreciated its value because they had had so little. Teklunia never went to school at all; she was taught some reading and writing by her father. Yet now she reads both Polish and English quite fluently. Felek went to school two winters but he reads constantly and writes beautiful letters. He believed education was very important -- but not for girls. For his sons he would have done anything in the world, made any sacrifice, to put them through school. For his daughters – why go to high school? You'll finish at 18 and get married. What good will high school be then? Music lessons, yes (you might attract a better man) but high school for a girl -- no!

They did not read stories to their children, but many an evening was spent in reminiscences of "The Old Country," personal experiences, history, legends. Felek knew many poems and songs and shared them and taught them to his children. He knew these little poems which mentioned boy and girls with the same names as his children. What embarrassment to his daughter when she recited one of these poems in school and learned that the name of the girl in the original poem was not the same as hers!

Holidays were observed in a traditional Polish manner. "Oplatek" at Christmas, "pisanki" at Easter, Herring, beet soup and the rest for Wigilia Supper, white "barszcz," eggs and home-grated horseradish for Easter breakfast. On Christmas Eve, some Polish-Americans left an empty place at the table for the Christ Child. Not they. Rather, they invited someone to share their meal: a bachelor uncle, a lonely neighbor, a widowed friend. This was proverbial Polish hospitality: "Gosc w dom, Bog w dom" (a guest in the home, God in the home) and "Czym chata bogata, tym rada" (what the cottage is rich in, that it is happy to share). All this and more was observed. American customs were quickly and happily accepted. Santa Claus, Halloween (pennies for the beggars), Thanksgiving turkey, Mother's Day, Father's Day, Decoration Day, Fourth of July.

Their ties to Poland remain. Letters are still exchanged regularly. They help their families with packages and money. They are interested in the political situation. They reminisce often. Their children are grown and they have been financially secure for a good number of years. A trip to Poland is within their means and has been suggested often, but they refuse. For one thing, they think that they would be overcome with emotion. The sight of those remembered fields and forests, wayside shrines and stork nests, the village church and cemetery, the family cottage with its thatched roof, the people and the sounds of their regional speech would overwhelm them. "We would not come back, we would die there!" Besides, when they left Poland it was without any thought of returning: it was not in their plans. They are content.

Despite the bad times, when they had to struggle, when they had difficulty making ends meet, through illnesses and worries, America has been good to them. Although they are proud of their Polishness, they are now Polish-Americans with the accent on American.

Their unspoken but instinctive motto is the same as that of another Polish-American, Arthur Rubinstein: "Nie dam sie!" In his autobiography, *My Young Years,* Rubinstein writes that he adopted this motto early in his career, when he was experiencing various trials and problems. Translated loosely and weakly it means, "I won't give in!" He did not. They did not.

At the ages of 80 and 83, they are still true to their unspoken motto. They will not give in to old age, to aches and pains, to loneliness. They are still active, still independent, still determined to make their own decisions and live their lives in their own way. "Nie dam sie" is a good motto. With love, admiration and deepest respect I, their daughter, accept that motto and recommend it to my children-their grandchildren.

POLISH NUT FILLED BUTTER HORNS

2 pkg. yeast	1 Tbl. sugar
¼ c. lukewarm water	1 tsp. salt
½ c. sour cream	1 c. butter or margarine
2 egg yolks	Confectioner's sugar
4 c. all-purpose flour	

Dissolve yeast in water. Let stand 5 minutes then stir. Scald cream, cool to lukewarm. Blend in egg yolks. Add the yeast. Sift flour, sugar and salt into mixing bowl. Add butter and blend in mixer until mixture resembles cornmeal. (If a food processor is available use it!) Add yeast mixture and mix thoroughly. Cover and chill several hours. Since this is a rich dough it rises very little. Divide dough into eight parts. Shape each piece into a ball. Roll from center into an 8 inch circle on a board sprinkled with confectioners sugar. Cover each circle with a thin layer of filling. Cut into 8 wedges and roll up beginning at rounded edge. Place on ungreased cookie pan; bake in a pre-heated oven without further rising. Cool slightly and sprinkle with sifted confectioners sugar. Makes 64.

Filling

2 egg whites	1 c. sugar
1 tsp. vanilla	1 c. finely chopped nuts
1½ grated orange rind	

Beat egg whites to soft peaks. Add sugar gradually, vanilla and orange rind. Beat until stiff. Gently roll in nuts. (If desired omit orange rind and add ½ tsp. cinnamon.)

*　　　　*　　　　*

By Maxine Walaskay

PIEROGIE

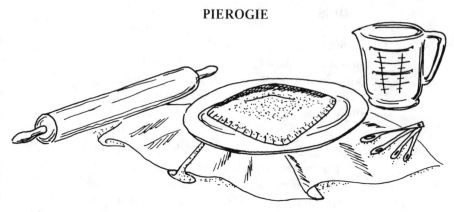

Pierogie Dough:

6 c. flour	1 c. milk
1 stick margarine	1 c. warm water
2 level tsp. salt	2 eggs

Melt one stick margarine in 1 c. water. Add 1 c. cold milk making sure liquid is lukewarm before proceeding. Add 2 eggs and beat well. Add 6 c. of flour and 2 tsp. salt. Knead until smooth and slightly glossy appearing.

Filling:

1 large onion diced	5-6 potatoes
2-3 tsp. butter	1 8-oz. container cottage cheese
Salt and pepper	

Peel and cook potatoes. Mash until all lumps are gone. Saute the large diced onion in the melted butter and add to the mashed potatoes. Add cottage cheese; salt and pepper to taste.

To Make:

Cut the dough into manageable portions (about 3) for rolling out. Roll the dough to less than ¼ inch thickness on a floured pastry cloth. The dough will be quite stretchy but this quality allows you to place more filling in each pierogie envelope. Cut the dough into squares about 3x3 inches. Top a square of dough with a Tbl. sized

dollop of filling and over with an additional square of dough pressing the edges together to form a seal.

I have found the only satisfactory way to make these somewhat tricky critters is by using a raviloi cutter that cuts and seals the edges at one time. This is not a pizza cutter which is somewhat more available. Mine was a gift so I can't recall the source but I believe a restaurant supply house or a good cook shop ought to carry them. With the ravioli cutter, pierogi making time is reduced by about ½.

As you begin rolling out the dough place a large kettle of salted water on to boil. Place the completed pierogi into the lightly boiling water about 3 at a time and cook until they rise to the surface. Remove with a slotted spoon. Pierogi may be eaten at this point if you like.

I prefer to keep out a family sized portion for frying, the next day. Place the finished periogi on a sheet of waxed paper on a cookie sheet. Freeze individually between sheets of waxed paper. As they become solid remove them and store in the freezer in a plastic bag. Otherwise, by freezing in one step you will have created an unmanageable lump of pierogie which is never ready to cook when you're ready to eat.

For serving: You can steam them, reboil, or fry pierogi for serving. To fry them, saute whatever quantity of onions you like until lightly golden in color and add the completely thawed pierogis into the frying pan. Cook these also until lightly golden. Season with salt and pepper to taste and serve 3 to 4 per person (the minimum if they happen to be Polish) with a dollop of sour cream for each pierogi.

If I make this once a year in November we are able to have some Christmas Eve and the day after Thanksgiving, plus one or two winter meals in Janaury. I save it for the bitter cold days as a sure cure for mid-winter blahs. Besides with all the onions who could get a cold?

*　　　　*　　　　*

BARSHCH

Beef soup bone (and or 1-2 lb. beef chuck)	1 can tomatoes
	3-4 fresh beets or can of beets
1 medium onion	1 tsp. sugar
3-4 celery stalks	1 Tbl. lemon juice
3-4 carrots	1 pt. sour cream

Prepare beef stock with soup bones, onion, celery stalk or tops, and several carrots, salt and pepper. Simmer about 3 hours. If you want a superb company dish add 1 or 2 lbs. beef chuck, that has been cubed.

When meat is tender remove vegetables (they will be over-cooked) and add 1 can tomatoes, and a wedge of thinly sliced cabbage. Peel and grate 3 or 4 fresh beets and add to the soup. Simmer 3 to 5 minutes. Season with tsp. sugar, 1 Tbl. lemon juice, salt and pepper to taste. Serve with dollop of sour cream.

Potatoes can be added small and whole if you want to fill up. Or, you may grate 2 beets and add a can of small whole beets. There are many ways to make this dish.

Serve with: Dark Rye bread and butter.

You really don't need much else. Its all in the pot and has the most beautiful color! You can get addicted.

*   *   *

POLISH CUCUMBER

2 medium cucumbers peeled	¼ tsp. sugar
	1 medium thinly sliced onion
1½ tsp. salt	
1 c. dairy sour cream or half and half	2 Tbl. vinegar
	1/8 tsp. black pepper

Cut cucumbers in thin slices. Add onion and sprinkle with 1 tsp. salt. Let stand 10 minutes and then press out excess liquid. Mix cream or half and half and rest of the other ingredients. Pour over cucumbers and onions and mix lightly. Chill about 2 hours.

POLISH SAUSAGE
(Kielbasa)

10 lb. ground pork	2 oz. salt
1 oz. pepper	1 medium size onion
¼ c. marjoram	Casings

Wash casing with cold water. Crush marjoram with hands and add to ground meat. Add salt, pepper and onion. Mix well and put in casings.

*   *   *

POLISH SAUSAGE PLATTER

1½ lb. pork sausage (links) cut in 12 pieces	1½ tsp. salt
6 slices bacon cut in 1 inch pieces	2 tsp. sugar
1 large onion sliced	¼ c. water
1 c. beer	1/8 tsp. pepper
1 medium cabbage, sliced	2 Tbl. flour
	6 hot boiled potatoes

Panfry bacon in Dutch oven until crisp. Remove to absorbent paper. Pour off all but 1 Tbl. drippings. Add sausage, onion and beer and cook slowly 15 minutes. Add cabbage, sugar, salt and pepper. Cook 15 minutes longer. Blend flour and water, stir into sausage and cabbage and cook until thickened. Fold in bacon. Serve on hot platter with boiled potatoes.

*   *   *

By members of the St. Marys Ladies Rosary Society of Bronson, including Jane Barry, Edna Kibiloski, Mary Kowalski and Irma Sarnovsky.

POLISH DOUGHNUTS
(Poczki)

1 yeast cake	1 c. sugar
3 eggs	½ c. oil
1 tsp. salt	2 c. milk

Dissolve the yeast in ½ c. lukewarm water. Combine milk, sugar, salt and oil and heat. When lukewarm add the yeast and the eggs, well beaten: add flour enough to make a stiff dough. Mix well and beat hard. Cover and let rise until double in bulk. Turn out on a floured board, roll out to 1/3 inch thick. Cut out, cover and let rise until double. Fry in deep hot lard.

*   *   *

CHRUSCIKI

3 c. flour	¼ lb. melted butter
3 whole eggs	¼ tsp. salt
4 yellows of eggs	1 shot glass rum
½ c. sugar	1 tsp. baking powder

To the sifted flour add whole eggs, yellows, sugar, salt and baking powder and melted butter. Also shot glass of rum. Work well and knead until dough does not stick to kneading board. Roll out and cut into 4x2 inch strips. Cut hole in middle of each strip, then pass one end of the strip through it to make a knot. Leave dough on board for ½ hour so it will dry lightly and then fry in hot lard. Take chrusciki out with fork and drain on paper towels. When cool sprinkle with powdered sugar.

*   *   *

HOMEMADE SAUERKRAUT

You need roughly 5 lbs. of cabbage for every gallon of your crock. For instance: a 10-gallon crock would need about 50 lbs. of cabbage.

Quarter cabbage and shred finely. Place 5 lbs. shredded cabbage and 3½ Tbl. pickling salt in large pan. Mix well with hands. Pack gently in large crock, using a potato masher to press it down. Repeat above procedure until crock is filled to within 5 inches from the top.

Press cabbage down firmly with potato masher to extract enough juice to cover. Cover with clean cloth. Place a plate on top and weight it down with a jar filled with water.

Keep crock at 65 degrees to ferment. Check kraut daily. Remove scum as it forms. Wash and scald cloth often to keep it free from scum and mold. Fermentation well be complete in 10-12 days. (If no bubbles rise, fermentation has ended).

Pack in hot, sterilized jars to within 1 inch from top. Add enough juice to cover. If you need more juice, make a weak brine by combining 2 Tbl. salt and 1 qt. water. Cover, screw band tight. Process in boiling water bath 15 minutes. Fifty pounds of sauerkraut makes about 15 qts.

*   *   *

RAW POTATO DUMPLINGS
(Kluski Kartofle)

8 large potatoes, grated	1 egg
1 large onion, grated	Salt and pepper to taste

Mix all things together. Add flour to thickness so can be dropped from hot spoon into boiling salted water. When dumplings rise to top they are done. Drain.

*   *   *

The Mathematics of a Mole

The mine dominated the lives of all the men, women and children who lived in the neighborhood. Whole families were common, and boys often went to work at an early age, a procedure made necessary to provide sufficient for the family needs.

There was never a complaint of the hardness of their labor. Whenever their spirits were dampened it was because a lag in the industry prevented sufficient employment. That "a miner has nothing to lose" and that he is "never broke till his neck's broke" were proverbial sayings once very familiar to Cornishmen.

It is a matter of frequent comment that mines where Cornish labor predominates are singulary free from strikes, lockouts, and disputes, which from time to time occur in almost all other industrial areas. Probably foremost among the reasons for the peaceableness of the Cornish miner was the "contract" system of wages under which he habitually worked. The men made their own contracts, and their pay depended upon the amount of rock broken. It is easy to see how different from that of the ordinary weekly wage the effect of this system must have been upon the men. A good pay-day depended upon the miner's skill, energy, and judgment and not on any decision of a wage board. If a contract was entered into and the conditions became adverse, the rock hard, and the lode narrow, it was not any employer that was to blame. On such occasions when his earnings were "slight", the Cornish miner simply hoped for a more bountiful nature and a better contract for the next month. This system tended to inculcate an extraordinary skill and judgment in his calling and to create an independence characteristic of his forefathers for many generations before him.

Nearly all of the shift bosses and mining captains rose to their positions from the ranks of the miners. They were in consequence able to appreciate the attitude of the miner and to deal fairly with

By James Fisher   (Prof. Fisher, now deceased, was dean of faculty at Michigan Technological University in Houghton and former head of the department of mathematics and physics.)   Reprinted from "Michigan History Magazine." July, 1945.

both him and the company when it became necessary to adjust contracts. The method of dealing with the men was generally extremely effective and though the position of a young captain newly raised to the rank was not, on the face of it, and easy one, eminent good sense and judgment on his part usually outweighed any jealous feelings.

The mine which provided work and wages for its employees when in health attended to them also in sickness and death. Each company of importance had its own mine doctor and at the larger mines its own hospital. The men contributed a fixed sum per month out of their wages, in return for which they and their families were entitled to attendance from the doctor and free dispensation of the necessary medicines. The usual amount deducted from the monthly pay at the mine office was fifty cents for single men and one dollar for married men. The amount collected was independent of the size of the family and in general paid for only a small part of the service rendered.

The miners and their families lived in houses provided by the companies, rent for which was deducted from the miners' monthly pay. For a great many years the rent collected was two dollars per month. The company kept the houses in repair, replaced broken window glass, and looked after the painting and decorating. The rental rate was increased in later years to a dollar per room per month, but even at the increased rate the companies were contributing liberally toward the comfort of their employees and their families in providing excellent housing conditions.

The fact that most of the mines followed the practice, prevalent in Cornwall, of contributing money for the amusement of the men and their families, indicates clearly enough the personal and friendly relationship between employers and employed. Local bands were equipped with instruments, and the players were allowed time concessions for their practices and concerts. Cornish wrestling matches, hammer and drill contests, carol singing at Christmas time, all helped to amuse and entertain the populace and provided a vent for the energetic "Cousin Jack."

Most Cornishmen are deeply and enthusiastically religious. The system of "local preachers" trained many of the miners to be both fluent and original speakers. A considerable number were miners throughout the week and preachers in the chapels on Sunday. They could deliver eloquent, earnest sermons without book or note and in the same natural tone of voice with which they might address their fellows on the street. Being in direct contact with all the problems which beset his honest hard-working comrades, he could speak in the exact terms and language of his hearers, and convince them that he thoroughly believed in the truth of what he said. How and when the local preacher found time to acquire the knowledge that he possessed is a mystery. To listen to such a preacher give an extempo-

Mining Michigan Ore   *(Photo from Michigan State Photo Archives)*

raneous prayer, to hear his thrilling appeal, and the earnest utterances at times of the members of the congregation, not in set phraseology but in words called forth by the nature of each petition, such as "Glory to God", "Amen", "Thanks to Him" showed that the worshipers, entirely oblivious to their surroundings, followed and sympathized with their spokesman and thus made his prayer their own.

Nothing delighted the old Cornish miner more than an evening at home or at the company store where he would work over the day's shift again in the presence of his family or of a few admiring neighbors. Especially would he boast of his own and his partner's skill in drilling in awkward positions underground. This was no empty boasting as anyone will affirm who has seen the work done. I have heard miners say "Single or double 'and 'tes all the same to he. 'Tes all the same, either 'and fore. Put the hole downright, cundit, cundit side tosser, breast hole or upper, he can beat 'im faster than any man in the parish."

It has been said that every Cornishman was born and bred with the conviction that he would one day make his fortune by speculating in the local mines. Many of the miners invested their small earnings in the mine which gave them work and in some cases fortune favored them. In any case their interest in the welfare and success of the mine was enhanced to the benefit of both the mine and the individual.

It has been said of the Cornish miners "that they possess the mathematics of the mole." Whatever that may be, the Cornishman seems to have an unusual sense of direction underground and also an unexplainable judgment as to where to look for the ore. As characteristically expressed, the "Cousin Jack" has a "nose for ore." Endowed with a species of instinct and an admirable judgment, they find means, practically, of not only locating lost lodes, but of solving certain problems which seem to demand all the calculation of geometry.

"However did you arrive at your results?" asked a mining engineer with some astonishment on one occasion when a working miner gave him the solution of a problem which he himself had trouble in figuring out with the aid of all the trigonometry at his command. "Why, Sir, replied the man, giving a slight nudge to one of his companions, "I tell 'ee I mizured 'im up brave and careful, and I found the length of un was two showl (shovel) hilts, three picks, a mallet, four lil' stones and so far as I cud spit, jus' zackly."

PASTIES

Crust for 9 or 10 pasties:

    8 cups flour
    1 lb. lard
    2 tbs. salt
    Add 1½ c. water - approximately

Ingredients for 1 pasty:

    1 c. potatoes
    Turnip and onions - add according to taste
    ¼ lb. pasty meat (pork and beef)

Roll enough crust to make a round piece the size of a 9 inch dinner plate. Place turnip, potatoes, onions, then meat on one half the crust (salt and pepper to taste). Put other half up over the ingredients and crimp edges together.

Bake at 375 degrees for about 1 hour.

*   *   *

CURRANT COOKIES

4 c. flour	1 c. white sugar
1 tsp. salt	¼ c. brown sugar
2 tsp. baking powder	½ tsp. nutmeg
Pinch of soda	1 c. margarine
½ c. currants - washed - add after mixing dry ingredients	

Mix as for pie crust. Add 2 eggs beaten with ½ c. milk. Roll out on floured board (¼ inch thick) and cut with cookie cutter. Bake at 375 degrees for about 12 minutes.

Collected by Beatrice Hosking of Nagaunee from some "good ole cousin Jacks," including Edith Hellier, Sally Kirby, Ruth Walimaa, Edith Hamton and Catherine Jenkins.

SAFFRON BUNS

8 c. flour	½ lb. margarine
1 c. sugar	2 Tbl. shortening
2 tsp. salt	

Mix these ingredients as you would pie crust. Then add:

½ pkg. currants
½ pkg. white raisins
Candied fruit if desired

Steep 1 pkg. saffron (1/16 oz.) in 1 c. boiling water - let cool. Set 2 pkg. yeast in 1 c. lukewarm water. Then add these and enough water to mix in all the flour and the saffron so that it is evenly distributed throughout the mixture. Let rise until double in bulk. Then make into buns and let rise again. Bake in a 350 degree oven for 35-40 minutes. Makes about 36 buns.

*   *   *

SUET PUDDING

3 c. flour	1 tsp. salt
1 c. suet (ground fine)	1½ c. water (approximately)

Mix all together and put in 9x9 inch pan. Bake ¾ to 1 hour at 350 degrees until crust is brown and crispy.

*   *   *

HEAVY CAKE

3 c. flour	1 tsp. salt
¾ c. sugar	½-¾ c. milk
2 tsp. baking powder	1 c. currants (rinse in boiling
1 c. shortening (work in like pie crust)	water

Pat dough into 9x13 inch greased pan, sprinkle top with sugar and bake 30 minutes in a 350 degree oven.

CHOW – CHOW

2 qt. green tomatoes	2 qt. cucumbers (peeled)
2 qt. small onions	6 red peppers
2 qt. green beans	3 large green peppers (cut both
3 qt. cauliflower	kinds of peppers in thin strips)

Wash vegetables then cut into coarse pieces. Put all in a quart aluminum pan, cover with 3 or 4 handfuls of salt. Leave over night, then drain off the brine in the morning. Place pan with the mixed pickles on the stove, adding one gallon of brown cider vinegar, also 4 Tbl. granulated sugar and 2 oz. of mixed pickling spices in a cheese-cloth bag. Simmer on the stove until the pickles are tender, but not mushy. When done, thicken with 2 c. flour, 4 oz. of tumeric powder, 4 oz. Coleman's mustard. Mix these dry first, then mix into a paste with vinegar. It is best to use one half and thicken the pickles, then use the other half, stirring with a wooden spoon, care being taken not to have it lumpy or burnt. When thickened enough, put in jars with tight lids. Makes about 22 pints.

*   *   *

PLUM PUDDING

2 eggs, beaten	½ lb. seeded raisins
1 tsp. salt	2 c. chopped suet
2 Tbl. molasses	½ pkg. currants (wash with
½ tsp. cinnamon	warm water)
½ tsp. ginger	2 c. flour
1/8 tsp. allspice	1 slice bread crumbs -
½ tsp. nutmeg	take off crusts
Dash of clove	Milk to make soft dough -
1½ tsp. baking powder	(can use water)
1 c. water	

Place in wet cloth to keep from sticking. Boil for 3 hours when made. Refrigerate. When ready to serve boil for 1 hour more. Keep covered in water at all times. Put a Tbl. salt in water. Also place saucer on bottom of pan when boiling so pudding won't stick.

Bread Dough at Four in the Morning

I recall returning to elementary school in the fall during the Depression and being asked to write a theme about summer vacation. My school mates wrote about Boy Scout camping trips, fishing with their uncles, motoring through the Rocky Mountains or the times they had at one of our beautiful Michigan lakes.

Sitting on the curb all summer watching the cars go by was my vacation. It did not occur to me then to value the long roll of Syrian bread, baked by my Lebanese mother, which I ate while I sat on the front porch or curb. In fact, I envied the other kids who had graham crackers for their snacks. Appreciation of these things perhaps requires a certain distance in time.

I could have written a unique theme about a mother who regularly rose once or twice a week at 4:00 a.m. to set her dough and bake the weekly bread. The early morning was prefered, for that particular bread baking required concentration and undisturbed attention. Individual rounds of dough were skillfully flattened, then rhythmically whirled and tossed in the air, finally coming to rest on a specially made flat pillow. This perfect, paper thin round, about twenty-four inches across, was then slapped onto a black iron sheet in the oven where it puffed like a balloon. At the exact moment it was removed, turned over, then returned for another few minutes. After it was done, it was placed on a white cloth on the table and the next loaf was begun.

In the early morning hours, silently and alone, my mother, like other Lebanese women, worked with a coordinated orchestration as regular and natural as breathing in and breathing out. Her work was truly an art. Each loaf was to her literally a prayer; each prayer a bead in a rosary of praise in thanksgiving to her creator, for her family, for her friends, for life itself.

By Fredric Abood (*Mr. Abood, the father of ten children, is a Lansing attorney specializing in criminal law. He is also on the faculty of Cooley Law School in Lansing.*)

133

The flat rounds of bread stacked up until there were two or three dozen. They were sprinkled lightly with water and wrapped in the large white cloth to become tender and chewy. Then, with the day dawning, the work was complete, just as the family was about to arrive in the kitchen. A certain portion of the dough was always saved for a special treat for them on baking days. The children came down to the sweet aroma of fresh bread and a platter of golden bits of dough deep fried in oil in a heavy iron skillet, then dipped in sugar.

I could have written a different theme about the unique entertainment my mother offered our family each summer. She gathered us together perhaps with a friend and we took a 'field trip' to some vacant lot or alley-way or riverside where the healthiest wild grape vines grew. With a great comraderie we picked bags of choice, young and tender grape leaves. After we had picked the grape leaves and brought them home, they were placed in a deep pan and soaked and washed. My mother would then prepare the meat which was ground by her with a coarse grinder, one of those that screws on the end of the table and is turned with a crank. The meat was cut in cubes, placed in the mouth of the grinder, and then shoved through to a coarse grind. She would then mix the meat with rice and spices and put the entire mixture in a pan on the table. After the leaves were thoroughly cleansed, we would place a spoonful of the mixture in a leaf, roll it and close the ends so that it was a tight cocoon around the meat, rice and spices. All this was artfully arranged in alternating rows in another pan over the lamb-shank bones which were saved to flavor the grape leaves.

Nor did I have the insight or imagination that would have delighted my ethnic classmates in writing about stuffed squash called "Koo-sa". A similar procedure as with the grape leaves, wherein the squash, from three to four inches, was hollowed by a vegetable borer specially made for this tricky feat. It was necessary to hold the squash and use the borer with a certain skill to get the walls of the squash the exact width without pushing a hole through the side. Again, the meat (ground coarse) with rice and spices was used to stuff the squash. The squash was then placed in a pan over lamb bones and cooked in tomatoes. Everyone in the family participated in this effort. The squash, of course, was home-grown in our garden.

I may have felt denied at the time not to have graham crackers, candy bars, and ice cream cones. I took for granted the "delicacies" which adorned our table daily: the never-absent bowls of large shiny black and tangy green olives, the nutritious creamy white "leban" which was served either hard or soft, as a sauce or as a spread for the Syrian bread. Leban is a white thick yogurt; Lebany is the white thin yogurt. Made each week with fresh milk from a starter, this traditional Arabic delight gave us food for thought as well. Since all Lebanese women were always willing to share their yogurt to have another portion made, there was no danger of breaking the chain. Who made the first leban? What started the first starter? Like the chicken or the egg, we visualized the long descent of leban down through history, for we were told the leban we ate was from an unbroken chain from that which Jesus' mother made in the Holy Land.

The unappreciated staple fare on our daily tables were dishes made from today's much-touted health foods; lentils and cracked wheat (Juddarah). My mouth may have watered a bit as I watched the men of the family eat their pork chops. Meat was not "family" food during the Depression.

Although I have no memories of games or toys or books in our home, nor was it furnished with any luxuries, it was in no way an empty or a joyless home. For the conversation and laughter of friends and relatives filled it constantly. Hospitality was a way of life. Welcoming and cherishing those friends was perhaps the one priceless possession we had. They stayed in touch with themselves by being genuinely close with their friends. No matter how often they were rejected and scorned in a society which laughed at their ill-fitting, hand-me-down clothes or their poor language skills; no matter how frequently that society offered them only menial, degrading jobs, they did not lose the sense of their innate dignity for they honored each other in their homes. They greeted and served one another like royalty. They felt valued and cherished because they truly were. Denied the entertainment of movies and television, they enjoyed the real pleasure of one another's company.

CRACKED WHEAT SALAD
(Saf-soof)

Cracked wheat is available in health-food stores and at groceries specializing in Middle and Near Eastern foods. For this recipe, use finely-cracked wheat.

Ingredients to serve 6
- 1 c. fine cracked wheat
- 1 cucumber
- 3 tomatoes
- 1 green pepper
- 1 bunch green onions
- 1 large bunch parsley
- 1 head of Romaine lettuce
- 1 bunch fresh mint (or 2 Tbl. dried)
- Juice of 3 lemons
- ½ c. olive oil
- 1 tsp. salt
- ½ tsp. peppercorns

Wash and crisp vegetables. Remove parsley leaves from stems, place leaves in a bowl of water, and refrigerate for several hours. Place cracked wheat in bowl, cover with cold water, and refrigerate for 1 hour before needed.

Cut all vegetables (except the lettuce) into very small pieces. Chop parsley; if green onions are not available, substitute a finely-chopped ordinary onion. If fresh mint is not available, use dried mint. Drain cracked wheat and squeeze by pressing between palms. Add to vegetables, pour dressing over, and mix well. Arrange large leaves of Romaine lettuce around platter and make a mound of the salad in the center.

Dressing: Mix lemon juice, olive oil, crushed peppercorns, salt, and mix well.

By Fredric Abood

THREE-CORNERED SPINACH PIE
(Fa-tyre Sa-ban-egh)

Ingredients to serve 4

    1 20 oz. package biscuit mix
    2 pounds fresh spinach (or 3 packages frozen chopped spinach, thawed)
    2 onions
    Juice of 3 lemons
    3 tablespoons pine nuts

Dough: Follow directions on biscuit mix to make soft dough. (Or mix 1 lb. all-purpose flour, 3 Tbl. olive oil, and warm water as needed to make soft dough, adding ½ cake yeast so that dough will rise.)

Stuffing: Wash spinach well (if frozen spinach is used, thaw). Drain well and press out all water. Chop spinach and onions and mix with lemon juice; the finer the consistency, the better. Add pine nuts.

Sprinkle board with flour, and roll dough with rolling pin to an even, Melba-toast thinness. Cut round 3-4 inch disks with cookie cutter or a glass. Knead dough leavings to make more disks until all dough is used. Arrange disks on floured board, place a Tbl. of stuffing in the middle of each, pick up 3 points of edge of dough at "natural triangle" and pinch firmly together in the center. This will make a "3-cornered pie." Arrange pies on buttered baking trays and bake on center rack of pre-heated, moderate 350 degree oven for 15 minutes. Serve cold.

*   *   *

KEBAB
(Kibbi)

This is the basic recipe for all kebabs. Using it, you will be able to make the many kebab variations that follow, each different in character. You can use either shoulder or leg of lamb.

1 lb. lean lamb, ground fine
1 c. cracked wheat
1 small onion
1 tsp. salt
1 tsp. whole black peppercorns
¼ tsp. powdered cinnamon

Wheat preparation: Pour cracked wheat into bowl; add just enough cold water to cover wheat and set bowl in refrigerator until you are ready to use it.

Meat preparation: If you grind the lamb yourself, first remove fat and gristle, cut into convenient chunks for grinding, and set aside. Crush peppercorns with salt in spice mortar until almost pulverized; mix in cinnamon and cubed onion, and then run together through grinder with the meat twice.

Remove cracked wheat from refrigerator, press between palms to squeeze out excess moisture, and mix with meat, kneading well. If mixture becomes stiff, dip your hands in ice water, and knead to soften. Run mixture through grinder again. You are now ready to serve or cook. Serves 4.

*   *   *

KEBAB PATTIES
(Kibbi Mi'lee)

These are simple patties, cooked as you would hamburger patties. Fry slowly in butter or olive oil. Serve with salad.

*　　　　　*　　　　　*

STUFFED SQUASH
(Qoosa Mih-shee)

There are many different sizes and varieties of squash. You want zucchini - as straight as possible, the size of small, plump cucumbers. Wash the squash, slice off the top, and core, leaving a ¼ inch shell, and taking out all the seeds. Be careful not to break the shell. I find a a grapefruit knife most effective.

Ingredients to serve 4
>½ c. raw rice
>1½ pounds ground lamb
>1 tsp. salt
>½ tsp. whole peppercorns
>¼ tsp. allspice
>8 squash
>1 large fresh tomato
>A few bones
>1 medium can tomatoes (about 17 oz.)

Mix uncooked rice with ground lamb in bowl. Add salt, crushed peppercorns and allspice. Stuff squash with this rice and lamb mixture, but do not pack too tightly: allow room for rice to swell in cooking. Cut fresh tomato into 8 pieces and stuff the opening of each squash with a tomato wedge. Now arrange squash over bones at bottom of kettle. Add canned tomatoes. Place an inverted dish over to hold squash down. Cover kettle and cook over medium heat 45 minutes. Serve hot.

Sojourner Truth -- Feisty Freedom Fighter

I told Jesus it would be all right
If he change my name. -- Negro Spiritual

Woman. Black. Old, nearly sixty years. Nothing much in 1856, wouldn't you say? Nevertheless . . .

It was Sojourner Truth, an old black woman who brought Battle Creek its first national attention by the simple act of choosing it for her home.

She had come to attend a Friends of Human Progress meeting October 4, 1856, to lecture anyone who would listen to her arguments for antislavery, women's rights and temperance. With her deep, penetrating voice---sad, bewitching, mystic---she did what she could to lift the downtrodden to human dignity. Her singing on that occasion was described and her first speech in the Quaker Meeting House reported in the *Anti-Slavery Bugle,* a weekly newspaper published in Salem, Ohio. The following summer she bought a house in Harmonia, six miles west of Battle Creek, moving into town ten years later.

Her beginning had not been promising. She was born to Negro slaves of the Hardenburgh family in New York's Ulster County near the Hudson River, about 1797. Her given name was Isabella, her surname changing with her owners. New York slaves were freed in 1827 and in the next few years Isabella had many rough experiences during which her faith and courage grew and grew. She was involved in two court cases which she won. By 1843 her five children were on their own and she started out to use her newfound talent of speaking, becoming a sort of tramp evangelist. Because she would preach the Lord's truth, she chose Truth as a new surname. When asked to

By Bernice Bryant Lowe

Reprinted with permission from "Tales of Battle Creek" by Bernice Bryant Lowe, copyright 1976 by Kimball House Historical Society. Originally titled "Sojourner Truth."

tell her first name, she abandoned Isabella, saying she would sojourn wherever she was needed, and call herself Sojourner Truth.

This woman could neither read nor write nor do any but the simplest arithmetic. She was, however, brilliant. Her vocabulary was large, her speech forceful, her voice lowpitched and vigorous. Audiences of all kinds felt her power. Yet her effectiveness came chiefly through her wit, her quick and clever banter, and droll humor. Actually, she was a philosopher with a childlike religious faith. She composed proverbs and, with her prodigious memory, enthralled those she had heard to serve her purpose. To anyone resigned to a sad fate or indulging in self-pity she used a sixteenth century adage. "Every tub has to sit on its own bottom." Even the least fortunate knew what she meant.

She often spoke in parables. In the early 1850s, after passage of the Fugitive Slave Law, there was a strong division between the Freesoilers, who advocated freedom for slaves but with limitation, and Garrison's followers who sought to abolish slavery. Sojourner said she could not explain very clearly the difference between Freesoilers and Garrisonians but she could *feel* the difference. "I remember seeing folks hackle flax," she said in her deep resonant voice, while circling her arm in a flailing gesture first slowly, then fast. "Some worked by–the–day, by–the–day, and others worked by the job, by the job, by the job, job, job. Freesoilers work by––the–day but the Garrisonians work by the job, job, job."

Sojourner had no formal education. She had the Bible and newspapers read to her, preferably by children because they inserted no comments and let her think out her own interpretations. Even though Sojourner depended upon listening for her education, her grasp of words and her memory were remarkable. She made understandable mistakes which her friend, Parker Pillsbury, called her 'rude eloquence.' Her Dutch accent from the language she spoke with her first owners until she was sold to English-speaking owners at about the age ten, may have contributed to her audience's delight.

Her parable of the weevil that was ruining the wheat in the early 1850s was told in a characteristic manner with her delightful use of an almost correct word. At the time, the antislavery workers were haranguing the United States Constitution as pro-slavery and anti-woman. Sojourner said, "Children,"(her audiences were always her children), "I talks to God and God talks to me. I goes out and talks to God in the fields and in the woods. This morning I was walking out and I saw the wheat a-holding up its head, looking very big. I goes up and takes a-hold of it. You believe it, there was no wheat there? I says, 'God, what is the matter with this wheat?' and he says to me, 'Sojourner, there is a little weebil in it.' Now I hears talking about the Constitution and the rights of man. I comes up and I takes hold of this Constitution. It looks mighty big and I feels for my rights, but there aren't any there. Then I says, 'God, what ails this Constitution?' he says to me, 'Sojourner, there is a little weebil in it.' " She lived to see the slavery weevil in the Constitution eliminated 15 years later.

Sojourner was also master of the quick retort. On a Battle Creek street she talked with a man who made it known that his station in life was far above hers. "Who are you, anyway?" she asked. Drawing himself up, trying perhaps to look as tall as the gaunt woman before him, he answered, "I am the only son of my mother." Sojourner looked disgusted and walked away after muttering. "I'm glad there are no more."

Somehow she used pathos without bitterness and managed to keep uppermost her sense of humor and her belief in the goodness of God. Her remarks sometimes had a lyrical quality. When her sight improved and she abandoned eyeglasses, she said, "The Lord has put new windows in my soul."

George Goodrich of Milton, Wisconsin, chided "Aunty Sojourner" for smoking a pipe even though she spoke for temperance. "The Bible says nothing unclean can enter the kingdom of heaven. A smoker's breath is unclean," he scolded. Continuing her puffing, she commented, "Brudder Goodrich, when I go to heaven I plan to leave my breff behind me."

Three books about her were published in her lifetime: in 1835, 1850 and 1875, the latter two going into further editions. Harriet Beecher Stowe, the Rev. Gilbert Haven, Gerrist Smith and others wrote and spoke about her and entertained her in their homes. She was a friend and coworker of antislavery reformers George Thompson of England, Wendell Phillips, William Lloyd Garrison, Parker Pillsbury, Frederick Douglass and of America's outstanding women's suffrage workers and many others interested in temperance and similar causes. Sojourner went into the Civil War refugee camps of former slaves in Arlington, Virginia, and accomplished so much in bringing them instruction in sanitation besides food, clothing and hope, that her work was financed by the Freedmen's Bureau.

PAN CORNBREAD

2 c. corn meal	2½ c. milk
1 c. flour	2 Tbl. sugar
1 tsp. salt	3 eggs
2 tsp. baking powder	3 Tbl. melted shortening

Mix together corn meal, flour, salt, sugar and baking powder. Stir in the milk. Beat the eggs together until light. Add the eggs to the bread mixture. Pour in most of the melted shortening. Grease pan with the rest of the melted shortening. Place in a heated oven at 375 degrees for about a ½ hour.

*   *   *

FRIED GREEN TOMATOES

4 medium size green tomatoes	½ c. shortening
1 c. corn meal	Season to taste

Wash and slice tomatoes, medium slices. Season with salt and black pepper, dip in corn meal, making sure tomatoes are well covered. Use heavy skillet. Let fat get hot. Brown tomatoes on both sides. Serve hot.

*   *   *

By Mother Waddles

Reprinted with permission from Mother Waddles Soulfood Cookbook by Mother Waddles, copyright 1970 by Perpetual Soul Saving Mission.

OLD FASHIONED MOLASSES BREAD

½ c. shortening
Black sorgum
Ginger
1¾ c. sugar

3 c. flour
Cinnamon
2 eggs
Buttermilk

Mix shortening and sugar until creamy. Add eggs and continue to cream (use mixer if you have one) then add milk and flour alternately. When ingredients are mixed, add cinnamon and ginger to taste and black molasses. Grease baking pan and bake at 350 degrees. May be served plain or iced with your favorite icing.

*   *   *

SWEET POTATO PUDDING — MARSHMALLOW TOPPING

3 sweet potatoes, medium
3 or 4 eggs
2 c. sugar, or more
1 can evaporated milk
1 Tbl. vanilla flavor

1 tsp. nutmeg
1 Tbl. lemon juice
½ stick butter or margarine
½ c. flour
1 Tbl. baking powder

Wash and boil potatoes with skins on. When tender to fork, take off fire, run cold water over them until cool enough to handle, then peel. Put in mixing bowl and mash with a potato masher. Add all ingredients except milk and butter and marshmallows. When ingredients are mixed, add milk gradually and beat as you add. Melt butter in baking dish. Pour in pudding mixture. Cook in preheated oven at 375 degrees. Lay marshmallows on top when done and put back in oven to brown.

*   *   *

CHITTERLINGS

After thawing chitterlings, place them in warm water, and take each chitterling one by one and cut out excess fat, and scrape out any grit that may be there. Wash thoroughly and put in heavy boiler with about 3 cups water. Add in:

Salt   2 small peppers
Black pepper   Lemon juice

Cover and put on medium flame until they start to cook and then turn flame low and let cook about 3 hours, stirring occasionally.

*   *   *

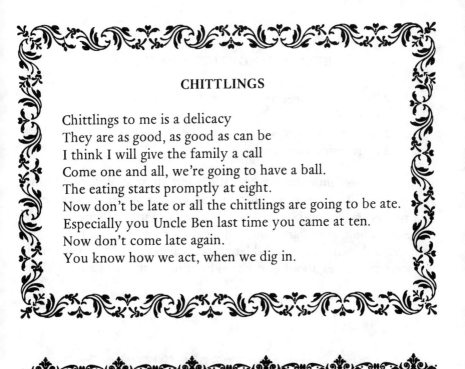

CHITTLINGS

Chittlings to me is a delicacy
They are as good, as good as can be
I think I will give the family a call
Come one and all, we're going to have a ball.
The eating starts promptly at eight.
Now don't be late or all the chittlings are going to be ate.
Especially you Uncle Ben last time you came at ten.
Now don't come late again.
You know how we act, when we dig in.

BAR–B–QUED PIG'S FEET

I'll bet that you didn't know that you could Bar-B-Que pig's feet. Well, I'll have you to know that they make a dish that's really a treat. Short of money, feeling kinda blue, let a meal of Bar-B-Qued pig's feet raise your spirits for you.

4-6 pig geet (cut in half - lengthwise)
Seasoning salt

Large onion
Cayenne pepper
Bar-B-Que sauce

Clean feet good, getting all hair off. Put on to cook. Put in onion and seasoning. Let cook until half done, about 45 minutes. Take out and put in shallow pan inside down, cover with sauce and bake in oven 350 degree until done.

*　　　*　　　*

BEEF AND NORTHERN BEANS

2 lb. boneless beef or stewing beef
1 lb. northern beans
1 large onion chopped

½ c. tomato paste
Seasoning salt
Black pepper

Cut beef into size desired. Wash and put in boiler. Pick beans and wash. Add to meat in boiler, put in enough water to be at least two inches above food. Add chopped onion. Put on flame. When it comes to a boil, turn flame low and let cook slow, about 1 hour. Season and add tomato paste and let cook until done. Add a little water if necessary. Takes about another ½ hour or 45 minutes after adding paste.

*　　　*　　　*

Settling in Detroit

The earliest Ukrainian immigrants began arriving in America in 1873 and the first Ukrainian family, that of Michael Stefansky, came to Detroit in 1897. Soon after, other families began to arrive, either directly from Ellis Island, New York, or from other cities in which they had lived for awhile. The peak of the first period of immigration was from 1901-1914. These Ukrainians were of the peasant class, driven from their homelands because of economic conditions and established themselves in Detroit and the surrounding suburbs as farmers, laborers and small businessmen. They settled in two distinct districts: East Side – in and around Hamtramck and North Detroit; and West Side – along Michigan Avenue from Livernois out, past Dearborn and from McGraw to Fort Street. They established churches, classes in their native tongue, community centers and all kinds of organizations in which they could hand down their customs, folklore, music and language to the new generation. They were happy in their new country, valued their new-found freedom very highly, enjoyed their economic independence tremendously and began to strive for a higher level of cultural and educational goals for themselves and their children.

From 1922 on, a second group of Ukrainian immigrants began settling in our city, who were more educated, with a number of professionals among them. They settled in the already established Ukrainian districts of the East Side and the West Side and joined in the activities of the community. There are definite traces of an upswing in the cultural movement and the Ukrainians began to hear and enjoy more classical Ukrainian songs, drama and literature -- but the movement was still not very widespread. It was not unusual for Ukrainian families to talk about sending their children to college, at this time, and a number of Ukrainians established and still operate

---

By Michael and Martha Wichorek

Reprinted with permission from "Ukrainians in Detroit" by Michel and Martha Wichorek, Printed by Michael and Martha Wichorek, 1968.

very successful businesses. These Ukrainians, along with the former immigrants continued to build, organize and improve Ukrainian community life. They spread far and wide so that today, we have large numbers of Ukrainians in all the neighboring suburbs and cities. More than ever, during this period, the total Ukrainian population was proud to be a part of the country that permits a man to become whatever his ability and initiative allow – this was truly the "land of opportunity, unlimited".

After the close of World War II, a third tide of Ukrainian immigration began to flow into the city. The highly educated professionals of Ukraine, driven from their homes by the enemy and herded into Displaced Persons camps all over Europe, were brought to Detroit on assurances of friends and relatives, the United Ukrainian-American Relief Committee, the Ukrainian Greek Catholic Committee for Refugees, or the Church World Service.

These latest arrivals, as those who came before them, settled wherever Ukrainians lived and congregrated, and are a very valuable addition to Ukrainian community life. They have brought with them the highest kind of Ukrainian culture and are working with new-found helpers, to place Ukrainian culture on par with world culture. Because their knowledge of the English language was limited, very few of them could obtain placement in the field of their specialty or profession. As a result, many doctors, artists, musicians, etc. had to work as common laborers, janitors and dishwashers while attending English classes in the evenings and on Saturdays. Many of this group have since become firmly established in Detroit universities, medical offices and positions of note, have become citizens of the U.S. and are truly a tremendous asset not only to the Ukrainian population, but, even more so, to the City of Detroit.

*　　　　　　*　　　　　　*

Christmas Eve is the most important time of the Christmas holiday season among Detroit Ukrainians. Even the second and third generation Ukrainians have learned to celebrate and enjoy Christmas as did their forefathers in Ukraine.

The day before Christmas is a strict fast day -- no food is eaten until SVIAT VECHEER, the Holy Supper. The entire family is home early to help put the finishing touches to the important feast, which mother has already been preparing for at least two days. The twelve course dinner is prepared entirely without meat or dairy products. There are twelve dishes to symbolize the twelve Apostles who sat with Jesus around the Last Supper table. A clove of garlic is placed at each corner of the table or beside each place (symbolic -- to ward off illness). A large Kolach (tall round bread, decorated on top with braided dough) has a candle inserted in the center and is the table centerpiece. Often a cylinder of salt is placed beside the Kolach (symbolic of the good things, over and above the necessities, which give flavor and enjoyment to life).

At a very special SVIAT VECHEER, with possibly some American guests, hay is strewn on the table under the tablecloth as well as under the table in remembrance of the Christ Child, born in a manger. Also, a sheaf of wheat (Sneep or Deedookh) is placed in the corner of the dining room, in thanks for the blessings of the year.

At the appearance of the first star at sundown, all sit down to eat Christmas Eve dinner. The father leads all in prayer and starts with Kootya – the symbolic Christmas dish of the Ukrainians, which is cooked whole-grain wheat, served with honey, ground poppy seed and chopped nuts. Each person must partake of each dish -- if only a spoonful. Then any eleven of the following foods, depending on which region of Ukraine the parents came from: borsch (beet soup); cabbage soup; cooked, jellied, or stuffed and baked fish or fish gravy; herring; holubtsih (cabbage leaves stuffed with whole grain buckwheat or rice, then cooked or baked); pirohih or varennikih (cooked dumplings with a potato, sauerkraut or plum filling); stewed mushrooms with beets; cooked large beans; stewed onions with mushrooms; fruit compote (cooked dried prunes, apples, pears, apricots, etc.); homemade twist breads (kolach, babka, etc.); honey cake (medeevnik); poppy seed cake (mahkeevnik); prune-filled cakes (pahmpooskih); and khroost (flake pastry).

After dinner, all sing the traditional Kolyadih (classic Christmas church hymns) and Kilyadkih (Christmas folk carols), then to to church for Midnight Mass. They also attend Christmas Mass on Christmas morning. They great each other with "Khristos Razhdayetsyah!" (Christ is Born!) and reply "Slaveetih Yeho!" (Let Us Glorify and Praise Him!) for the entire Christmas season. Groups of carolers visit Ukrainian households during this season to sing Kilyadih, and on New Year's Eve, they add Schedrivkih (New Year's songs of hope, extending best wishes for success and good health in the coming year). All money collected for caroling is donated for charitable and other worthy projects.

JELLIED PIG'S FEET
(Drahli or Studenina)

3 pigs feet, split
   lengthwise
1½ lb. beef shank,
   center cut
1 Tbl. salt or to taste
1 whole carrot

2 stalks celery and leaves,
1 medium onion
1 clove garlic
5 to 6 peppercorns
1 bay leaf

Scrape, trim and wash pig's feet clean. Wash shank. Place feet and shank in a large kettle - add salt and cover with cold water. Bring to a boil, then skim. Cover and simmer VERY SLOWLY otherwise rapid boiling will make broth milky rather than clear.

After 3 hours of cooking, add whole vegetables and spices. Continue simmering until meat comes off bones easily. Cooking period will be about 6 hours.

Carefully remove feet and shank from broth. Remove all bones - cut large pieces of meat. Arrange meat in a suitable dish; dice cooked carrots and add to meat for color. Strain broth and season to taste, pour over meat. CHILL THOROUGHLY.

Before serving, remove fat from top and slice. Garnish with sprigs of parsley and lemon wedges.

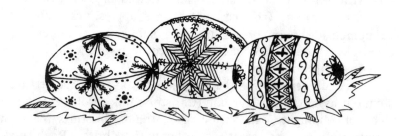

By Sophia Sofian Boan

SOUP

Soups, a mainstay in the Ukrainian diet, are served at nearly every meal. They can be hearty main dish soups to delicate broths.

Borsch is the national soup of the Ukraine. Mildly tart with beet predominating, it is made with a base of rich meat stock except during Lent and on Christmas Eve. There are several varieties of borsch, depending on regional and personal preferences and on the season.

A summer favorite version of borsch, mildly sweet, is made with fresh fruits such as cherries. This soup can be served hot or cold, clear or with vegetables.

An excellent accompaniment to borsch or broth is Vushka (little ears) which are tiny dumplings about the size of walnuts and filled with various kinds of fillings for example, meat or mushrooms. These little ears are joined at the corners and take their name form the shape.

*   *   *

BEAN SOUP

1 lb. navy beans, washed and drained	1½ c. diced celery with leaves
1 large smoked ham hock	2 cloves garlic, minced
3 medium potatoes, cooked and mashed	¼ c. finely chopped parsley
2 medium onions, chopped	Salt and pepper to taste

Cover beans with water and bring to a boil. Boil 2 minutes. Remove from heat, cover and allow to stand 1 hour.

Drain beans and measure liquid - add enough water to make 5 qts. Return beans to water and add ham hock. Bring to boil again and simmer covered for about 2 hours.

Remove ham hock and cut up meat. Return meat along with potatoes, onions, celery, garlic and parsley to stock. Cover and simmer 1 hour longer.

Season to taste with salt and pepper.

Beer bread is excellent with this soup!

BORSCH
(Meatless)

1 oz. dried mushrooms	3 c. water

1 medium onion, chopped	1 bay leaf, optional
2 Tbl. oil	10 peppercorns
2 medium beets, chopped	1 Tbl. vinegar or lemon juice
1 carrot, chopped	2 Tbl. tomato paste
1 stalk celery, chopped	1 c. chopped cabbage
6 c. boiling water	1 medium onion, whole

Simmer mushrooms in water for 1 hour. Strain and save stock. Rinse mushrooms and set aside.

Saute chopped onion in oil. Add beets, carrot and celery and cook 5 minutes. Add 6 cups water, whole onion, bay leaf, peppercorns, vinegar and tomato paste. Cook 15 minutes. Add cabbage and simmer 20 minutes. Remove the whole onion, peppercorns and bay leaf. Add mushroom stock and salt to taste.

Cool to let flavors mellow. Serve hot or cold. Add mushrooms and a dollop of sour cream to each serving. Vushka or little ears may be served with borsch.

Tastes better a day or two later!

*   *   *

BEER BREAD

3 c. self-rising flour	1 can (12 oz.) warm beer
3 Tbl. sugar	

Stir together flour and sugar. Mix in beer, stirring only until all ingredients are moistened. Turn into a 9x5x3 inch greased loaf pan.

Bake in 350 degree oven 55 to 60 minutes or until knife inserted near center comes out clean.

Variation - Add ½ cup raisins.

VUSHKA WITH MUSHROOM FILLING
(Little Ears)

Filling:

These tiny dumplings may be filled with meat, fish or mushrooms.

1 small onion, finely chopped	2-3 Tbl. butter
2 c. chopped cooked mushrooms	2 egg yolks
	Dill weed, optional

Saute onion in butter, do not burn. Add mushrooms and cook until tender. Season.

Remove mixture from range and beat in egg yolks. Dill weed may be added for flavor. Cool mixture thoroughly before putting into dough.

Dough:

2 c. all-purpose flour	1 egg
1 tsp. salt	2/3 c. cool water

Mix flour, salt and water, then knead lightly, cover with towel and set aside.

To Form Dumplings:

Roll dough thin on floured surface and cut into rounds (2-inches) or 1½ inch squares. Hold dough in palm of hand and place spoonful of filling in center. Fold in half. Press edges to seal, then lay on dry kitchen towel and cover.

To Cook:

Drop a few at a time into a large pot of boiling salted water. Boil rapidly about 3-4 minutes. Spoon into colander and rinse with hot water. Drain. Makes about 30 dumplings.

HERRING SALAD

Not only colorful but delicious as well...

2 c. pickled herring	1 Tbl. chopped onion
1 c. cooked diced potatoes	½ c. sour cream
1 c. cooked diced beets	2 Tbl. vinegar
1 tart apple, chopped	1 hard-cooked egg, sliced
1 dill pickle, chopped	Chopped parsley

Combine herring with potatoes, beets, apple, pickle and onion. Season with pepper.

Mix sour cream with vinegar and add to above. Toss salad ingredients lightly when adding the dressing.

Shape salad into a mound and garnish with egg slices and parsley.

*　　　　*　　　　*

YEAST RAISED MEDIVNYK

1 pkg. dry yeast	1 tsp. baking soda
3 Tbl. lukewarm water	1 tsp. cloves
2 c. honey	1 tsp. cinnamon
4 Tbl. butter	1 tsp. salt
4 eggs	¾ c. golden raisins
3½ c. sifted flour	

Sprinkle yeast over lukewarm water and let stand about 10 minutes. Bring honey to a boil, cool slightly. Add butter to honey and beat thoroughly. Cool to lukewarm. Beat eggs until light and combine with the honey mixture.

Sift all dry ingredients together three times. Stir some of the dry ingredients into the egg-honey mixture, add yeast and beat thoroughly. Stir in remaining flour.

Spoon batter into a well-buttered loaf pan, or spoon into a tall slim can for an attractive shape.

Bake about 1 hour in a 325 degree oven.

Farmers, Educators and Businessmen

If the Cornish immigrants had an "eye for ore" the German settlers had "eyes for the soil." In 1873, a Roman Catholic missionary noted that the Germans remained in Detroit just long enough to earn money to buy land outside the city and establish farms. In speaking of a German colony near Ann Arbor, the clergyman noted "their grain and cattle are unsurpassed in Michigan."

Like other early immigrants from European nations, the German settlers of 1840–50 sought a life of freedom in Michigan. Many came here to escape lengthy military obligations imposed upon each citizen in their homeland. These people, upon their arrival in America, quickly adopted the philosophy that the United States will be "my country, may she be ever right, but right or wrong, my country."

Like the settlers from New England, the Germans, too, had their "spies" or "scouts" which preceded the main immigrating party into a new area. Often the scouts' reports were very important in determining exactly where the colony would be established. This was the case when a group of fifty families living in the Saxonia Region of Germany were recruited by an agent to settle in an iron mining district of our Upper Peninsula. The scouts spent the winter of 1872 at a mining location prior to the main party's arrival from Germany in April 1873. However, when the main party reached New York in the spring, the scouts were on hand to tell them about what they considered to be unfavorable weather conditions in the Lake Superior area. The group promptly proceeded to Forestville in Sanilac County, purchased land, and became enterprising farmers in the fertile, southern Michigan agricultural community.

Michigan's German immigrants not only had an eye for the best farmland, but they also sought out the most desirable urban

By Dr. George P. Graff

Reprinted from "The People Michigan" by George P. Graff, 1974, Michigan Department of Education.

properties for their businesses. For example, Detroit's "German-town" was developed at the center of a growing city. Although Germans were reported "in considerable numbers" in Detroit as early as 1820, it was after 1848 that the growth of the German community really occurred. The peak of German immigration took place just prior to 1900. At that time "Germantown" extended out Gratiot Avenue from Broadway to beyond St. Joseph's Church.

Although thirst for learning was not exclusively a German attribute, these central European immigrants expressed through both printed and spoken words their desire for higher education. Many early teachers in Michigan's public schools either arrived directly from Germany or were of German-American descent. Our fundamental law on education as adopted by the Michigan Constitution was based upon the Prussian (German) System. The important aspects of this program included primary and secondary schools and a university, as well as public taxation and state supervision. Of course, these are still basic concepts in our present educational system.

The Germans not only excelled in the classroom, but applied theory in practical situations. Such was the German influence upon the development of Michigan's natural resources.

Names such as Orlman, Engleren and Fleitz were well known in the timber business and Brutung, Kaufman and Schlesinger capitalized on the iron market. It was John Cordes who developed the world-famous plaster quarries near Grand Rapids. Another German, Conrad Kuhl, was one of the earliest producers of salt in the Saginaw Valley. John A. Roebling, the German-born builder of the famous Brooklyn Bridge purchased the Tamarack and Osceola Wire Company at Dollar Bay in our Copper Country in 1912. The firm operated until 1939 under Roebling's ownership.

Other German names such as Hetler, Eggert, Rugrick and Weiss will not be found in Michigan history books. These families were farmers who grew fruit and berry crops on the small farms near Benton Harbor. Most of these farms were less that twenty acres but formed the framework for the famous Benton Harbor Fruit Exchange known throughout the nation.

During the years 1836 to 1839 many German Catholics settled the central Michigan area around Westphalia in Clinton County. After arriving in Detroit, they hired a guide and together they walked cross country to Westphalia.

Most of the fertile "Thumb Region" in Michigan was settled by Germans, often to the exclusion of other nationalities. Devout Lutherans or Roman Catholics, the German communities of Saginaw, Bay, Tuscola and Huron Counties reflected the traditions of the fatherland. The towns of Frankenmuth, Frankentrost and Frankenlust were originally German missionary colonies established to convert Indians. Until 1905 everyone in Frankenmuth was of German birth or descent except one Welshman and one Indian, and, as you might imagine, these two spoke German fluently.

The first German windmill in northeast Michigan was built in Rogers City in 1888. The wind, which turned the giant arms, provided the power needed to grind grain raised throughout Presque Isle County.

A county directory from anywhere in Michigan will show that the Germans have been instrumental in developing numerous communities. From the copper stamp-mill town of Freda in the Upper Peninsula's Houghton County to the towns of Steiner and Strasberg, 600 miles to the south near Toledo in Monroe County, the Germans have always been an influential factor in building Michigan.

Farming Michigan's Land   (*Photo from Michigan State Photo Archives*)

GERMANS FROM RUSSIA

To many, the term "Germans from Russia" prompts a quick response "Who?" "From Where?" "How Come?" Although these are perfectly natural expressions of surprise, it illustrates quite well how little most of us really know about this important segment of our German population.

Victor A. Reisig of St. Joseph, Michigan's foremost authority on this group, estimates that approximately 60,000 Berrien County's residents were either born in Russia or are the children or grand-children of Russian-born Germans. This means that about 85 percent of the Germans in southwestern Michigan came from Russia -- principally the Volhynia Province. In fact, Berrien County, Mich-igan, has the largest concentration of Germans from Volhynia to North America.

History records that from 1763 to 1861 over 23,000 Germans, mostly Hessians, moved to the Volhynia and Volga terri-tories of Russia. Catherine the Great, the German-born ruler of Russia at that time, promised these immigrants free land, full citizenship and the right to continue their German language. In addition, she assured them that they could continue their German customs and re-ligion, and, very importantly, would be exempt from military service. This region was considered "underdeveloped" and Catherine hoped that by inducing the hard-working Germans to settle in Russia they would serve as examples to her Russian citizens that this "waste-land" could be made productive. Actually the Germans settled in two distinct regions. The one closest to Germany was Volhynia, a province on the Polish-Russian border. Immigrants from this group later settled in southwest Michigan. Another group of Germans jour-neyed far to the east and settled in the Great Plains region near the Volga River. Settlers from this group later moved into our Saginaw Valley and the "Thumb Area."

Once in Russia, however, the Germans found that they were not allowed to practice their trades and careers as promised, but were told by the Russian government that they must become farmers. Al-though this must have been a shock to the skilled craftsman, they became farmers. In fact, these German settlers were among the best farmers Russia had ever seen.

By the 1870s serious problems developed between the Ger-man's and their Russian neighbors who never completely accepted the immigrants into their communities. Thus, the stage was set for another German migration.

Because of their ability to grow sugar beets and grain, it was natural that their "scouts" were sent to America where the Great Plains seemed to be an ideal place to continue their agricultural skills. These Germans from the Volga region of Russia, called "Volga Russians," introduced sugar beets into Colorado and other western states. Some of these Germans moved back to Michigan from the west and developed our sugar beet industry in the Saginaw Valley. In some instances, agents from Michigan sugar companies actually solicited immigrants by encouraging early settlers to write relatives to come to Michigan.

Victor Reisig reports that immigration Germans from Russia's Volhynin region literally took over the fruit and nursery farms in southwestern Michigan from 1890--1910. Then they became the sugar beet, peppermint, dill, cucumber and muck farm specialists between 1900--1930.

Most of the immigrants were of the Lutheran, Evangelical (Reform) or Roman Catholic faiths. Boys and girls today will approve of their observance of Christmas which lasted three days. These farm wives were expert cooks especially skilled in baking pies, cakes and various pastries. In the Sebewaing area of Huron and Tuscola counties a seasonal treat was "hollerstreibli." This was a deep-fried, pancake-like confection that was made from elderberry blossoms. In June and early July the large, white blossom-heads of the elderberry plant were gathered and tapped lightly to remove loose dirt. Washing was not permitted, since the small flowers making up the head would close and destroy the flavor. The heads were then dipped into a light batter made of eggs, milk, flour, a little sugar and a pinch of salt. Then they were deep fried until brown, drained and dusted with powdered sugar. As a dessert, it was served with coffee or tea.

Common first names of these German immigrants from Russia were Jacob, Gottfried, Gottlieb and Henry. Girls' and womens' names included Paulina, Maria, Emilia and Lydia. Their last names are among our most common German names: Bauer, Fischer, Goebel, Koehlor, Koch, Neumiller, Weber and Weiman.

BAKED POTATO SQUARES
(Kartoffelkasekuchen)

3 c. leftover or prepared
mashed potatoes
2 Tbl. flour
1½ tsp. salt
¼ tsp. fresh ground
pepper
½ c. sour cream

2 Tbl. chopped chives
1 egg, slightly beaten
½ c. Swiss cheese,
shredded
4 slices crisp bacon
crumbled

Mix potatoes, flour, salt, and pepper. Spoon into greased 9x9 x2 inch baking dish, spreading mixture to edges. Mix sour cream, chives, and egg; spread over potato mixture. Sprinkle with cheese and bacon. Bake in 350 degree oven 25 to 30 minutes or until set. Cut in squares. Serves 4 to 6.

*   *   *

MIXED VEGETABLE SALAD
(Gemuse Salat)

1 c. peas - cooked
and drained
1 c. cauliflower - cooked
and drained
1 can (4-oz.) mushroom
buttons, drained
1 c. asparagus - cooked,
drained, chopped

½ c. mayonnaise
½ c. plain yogurt
½ tsp. salt
1/8 tsp fresh ground
pepper
1 tsp. prepared mustard
2 drops hot sauce
Minced parsley

In large bowl combine peas, cauliflower, mushrooms and asparagus. Mix mayonnaise, yogurt, salt, pepper, mustard and pepper sauce; pour over vegetables and toss well. Garnish with parsley.

By Gloria Pitzer

Reprinted with permission by Gloria Pitzer, Secret Recipes, Box 152, St. Clair, MI 48079.

ROAST BEEF SALAD
(Rindfleischsalat)

3 c. diced cooked roast
  beef
About 2 small dill
  pickles, chopped fine
  (¼ c.)
½ small onion, minced
Minced parsley

½ c. mayonnaise
2 Tbl. wine vinegar
1 Tbl. oil
1 Tbl. prepared mustard
¼ tsp salt
1/8 tsp. pepper

In large bowl combine beef, pickles, onion and 2 Tbl. parsley. Mix mayonnaise, vinegar, oil, mustard, salt and pepper; pour over salad and toss well. Chill well. Garnish with parsley.   Serves 3.

*   *   *

FARMER'S OMELET
(Bauernomelette)

3 slices bacon, diced
1 large boiled potato,
  diced fine (1 c.) or
  1 c. macaroni
3 eggs

1 Tbl. water
½ c. shredded cheddar
  cheese
1/8 tsp. salt or to taste
Dash of pepper
Minced parsley

In an 8 or 9 inch skillet fry bacon and potatoes until bacon is crisp and potatoes are browned. Beat eggs and water slightly; stir in cheese, salt and pepper and pour over potato-bacon mixture. Cook over low heat until slightly set, lifting edges with spatula to allow uncooked egg to run underneath. Cook until set. Flip onto warm serving plate. Garnish with parsley. Serve at once. Makes 1 or 2 servings.

*   *   *

APPLE STRUDEL

1½ c. flour	Filling:
½ tsp. salt	6 c. sliced apples
2 Tbl. salad oil	¾ c. sugar
½ c. lukewarm water	2/3 c. raisins
¼ c. butter, melted	1 Tbl. cinnamon
2 Tbl. dry bread crumbs	Grated rind of ½ a lemon
¾ c. ground almonds	
1 lb. powdered sugar	

Measure flour, salt, oil and water into bowl. Mix with fork until all flour is moistened and dough cleans bowl. Turn dough onto lightly floured surface: knead until dough does not stick to surface and is satiny smooth, about 10 minutes. If necessary, sprinkle surface with small amount of flour while kneading. Shape dough into ball; brush with melted butter and cover with warm bowl. (To warm bowl, rinse with hot water, drain and dry.) Let test about 30 minutes - dough will be easier to handle.

While dough is resting, cover a space on counter or table about 3 feet square with large dish towel or tablecloth. Tuck ends of cloth under and secure with tape. Sprinkle cloth with small amount of flour. Assemble ingredients for filling but do not mix.

Heat oven to 425 degrees. Roll dough on cloth to 1/8-inch thickness. Place hands palms down and close together under dough; gently lift and move hands apart until dough is paper thin and is stretched evenly to form a 30 to 36 inch square. Trim thick edges with kitchen scissors.

Brush square with melted butter and sprinkle with bread crumbs. Sprinkle almonds in a 3-inch strip along one edge. Mix filling; spread over strip of almonds to within 2 inches of each end. Lift edge of cloth nearest apples with both hands; roll up square as for a jelly roll. Place roll seam side down on greased baking sheet in a horseshoe shape. Brush with melted butter.

Bake 15 minutes. Decrease oven temperature to 375 degrees. Bake until golden brown, about 15 minutes. Remove from oven; sieve confectioners sugar over top. Serve warm or cool.

A Covered Wagon to Hope

The following excerpt is from "Our Heritage–An historical Narrative," by Jette Pierce Lawrence of Climax. Written in 1957, Mrs. Lawrence traces her family from England to Rhode Island in 1765 and on to Michigan in the 1800s. In this particular passage, her grandparents are driving their covered wagon to southern Michigan to settle with their three small daughters. They have just taken a steamboat from Buffalo to Detroit.

It didn't take Orrin long to shake the dust of Detroit off the tailboard as he headed them into the first good road that he found leading west. He hoped to cover twenty-five miles before night. For the two girls bouncing around in the back of the covered wagon as they watched the slowly disappearing city fade from sight, the idea, to say nothing of the thought, that in a few years they would be traveling this very same road going the same way as newly wedded brides, never entered their minds. Aurilla, the baby, rode, of course, with Mama and Daddy on the seat ahead.

They stayed that night at an inn not far from Ann Arbor. It was a low rambling sort of structure. The next morning, as Orrin was paying his bill, he inquired, "What is the best road to Barry County? That is where we are headed, and how do we get there?"

As he reached for a map, the genial inn keeper said, "Well, sir, we will see," as he traced the route with a stubby finger. "The trail seems to follow the Kalamazoo River. It's an old Indian trail. After awhile it goes through Jackson, then on to Marshall. I understand that someone in the Legislature last year wanted to make Marshall the capital of the state, but that fell through. And only last year, 1847, Lansing was made the capital. Funny what men with a little power can do. Lansing isn't any place at all. Just a sort of mud hole. Where you branch off toward the northwest, you can make further inquiries.

"Good luck to you, sir, and to your little family. Fine girls you have there," remarked the inn keeper.

"Thank you for your help and good wishes." With these words, Orrin went out and climbed into the wagon beside Sally

Marie. Nothing much bothered Orrin ever. He was a complacent man, and some of this contentment was imparted to Sally as she snuggled down beside him and said, "I do hope you find some work there. Surely Uncle Rockwell would not have asked us to come on a wild goose chase." And with this comment Sally slid into a state of complacency herself. And the Loomis' were again on their way with the end almost in sight.

As they drove on, they passed some fields where wheat had been harvested and they drove around many swamps. Orrin said, "I'd like to trap and hunt here. This is a wonderful country for wild ducks and just look at the height of those muskrat houses, that means we will have a hard winter."

Then they came to a stretch of heavy virgin timber where sawmills had not yet moved in. "Did you see that big oak that we just passed? And look at that maple -- five feet through if an inch. Bet pigs would grow hams and bacon on the beechnuts around here." Orrin stopped the team so the girls could get out and walk. They picked wild flowers and picked up nuts, filling their sunbonnets. When tired, they climbed back into the wagon and exclaimed, "Daddy, we tried to put our arms around one of those trees, but the both of us couldn't reach each others hands. And look at those nuts. What kind are they?" And excitedly they showed Orrin their bonnets filled with shagbark hickory nuts.

They spent the next night in Marshall. There Aurilla became frightened at some black men because she had never seen any before. They were fugitive slaves being run through to Canada. Marshall was one of the underground railroad stations. At Battle Creek they left the Kalamazoo River Valley and headed into hilly country, not as bad as that which they had left in New York, however. After traveling almost all day, by inquiring, they found they were in Barry County. Now they must find Hope Township where Uncle Rockwell lived.

When Orrin reined the grays to a halt at Uncle Rockwell's cabin, Aunt Jerusha and Uncle Rockwell welcomed them with open arms. It was so good for all of them to be once again with their own kith and kin.

Although it had been only two years since the Pratts left New York, there was much for them to talk about. Rockwell had only that day filled the tick with clean fresh-smelling straw in honor of their coming. The trundle bed had been pulled out and a fresh straw tick put upon it, too, for Julia, Elizabeth and Caroline jumped in the middle of it and nearly sank from sight.

However, they did not intend to live forever off Uncle Rockwell, so one day Sally said to Orrin when they were alone, "Orrin, a man at the store said that an Isaac Pierce on Climax Prairie has a lot of land and I think it would be a good idea for us to go see if you cannot work for him."

"Well," answered Orrin, "I cannot go tomorrow. I've promised the girls I would take them fishing on Cloverdale Lake in the morning. Then I'll go see the storekeeper and learn more about that Pierce fellow."

And that is what he did. Orrin was satisfied for the girls caught some good bass.

One of the many nameless pioneer families who helped settle Mich-- igan. *(Photo from Michigan State Photo Archives)*

YORKSHIRE PUDDING

2 to 6 Tbl. drippings   1 c. milk
   from beef roast   1 c. sifted flour
2 eggs   ¼-½ tsp. salt

Heat an oblong pan and pour in beef drippings. Grease pan well with beef drippings and keep pan hot. Beat eggs well and add to flour and salt which have been sifted together. Slowly add milk to egg-flour mixture and beat with egg beater for 2 minutes. Pour batter into pan. Batter should be about ½-inch thick. Bake in hot oven at 450 degrees for 15 minutes. Reduce heat to 350 degrees and bake 15 minutes longer. Serve immediately with roast beef and gravy.
    Note: This can be baked in a 10-inch pie pan.

This is a wicked recipe for anyone watching cholesterol!

*   *   *

TEA

When you make tea, be certain you use fresh, cold tapwater and bring it to a boil. Rinse teapot with scalding water and empty the teapot immediately prior to making tea. Put in loose tea leaves and add boiling water. If tea leaves sit in a damp empty pot too long, they will develop a burned vegetable taste.
    The best ratio for making tea is one scant teaspoon of leaves for 5½ ounces boiling water plus one teaspoon for the pot (optional addition).
    Brew three to five minutes and stir or swirl tea leaves once during brewing. Strain tea into another heated pot. Serve with or without sugar or honey, add milk or cream or lemon if you wish.

By Millicent Lane

CRUMPETS

1 pkg. yeast	1½ tsp. salt
¼ c. lukewarm water	3 Tbl. shortening
1 c. milk	1 egg, beaten
2 Tbl. sugar	3 c. all-purpose flour

Soften yeast in lukewarm water. Scald milk and add to it the sugar, salt and shortening. Cool to lukewarm. Add egg and 2 c. flour and beat thoroughly. Add remaining flour. Turn out onto floured board and knead until smooth and satiny. Place in lightly greased bowl and grease surface lightly. Cover and allow dough to rise in a warm place for 30 minutes. Beat 3 minutes and repeat. Beat 3 minutes and let rise a third time.

After beating 3 times, bake dough at once by pouring batter into muffin rings set on a hot greased griddle. Fill rings about 1/3 full and allow them to bake without turning for about 20 minutes. Cool and toast and serve with butter and jam or marmalade. Makes about 1 dozen. Serve with Tea. Yum!

Note: *Beating makes the large holes characteristic of the crumpet.*

* * *

LANCASHIRE HOT POT

2 c. cooked beef or lamb in cubes	1½ lb. boiled potatoes, peeled and sliced
Salt, freshly ground pepper	2-4 oz. mushrooms quartered (optional)
2 Tbl. flour	1 c. hot beef stock
Prepared mustard	or bouillon

In greased 1½ or 2 qt. casserole, layer potato slices, meat, celery, and mushrooms (optional). On each layer of potatoes, sprinkle some salt, pepper and flour. Sprinkle about 1 tsp. prepared mustard on each layer of meat. Casserole should begin and end with potato layer. Pour one cup hot stock or bouillon over all. Cover casserole and bake at 350 to 375 degrees for about 35 minutes or until bubbly hot. Cover of casserole should be removed for about last 10 to 15 minutes.

Serves 6 to 8. (Great way to use leftovers)

VEGETABLES

Brussel Sprouts:

Cook 1 package frozen Brussel sprouts according to package directions using ½ c. chicken broth instead of water. Drain. Toss with 3 Tbl. butter, ¼ tsp. salt, dash of pepper, and 1 tsp. caraway seeds. Serve to 3 or 4.

Brussel Sprouts:

Cook frozen Brussel sprouts as package directs. Melt 3 Tbl. butter and cook over low heat until browned. Add 1 Tbl. lemon juice and some salt and pepper and pour over sprouts. Serves 3 or 4.

Baked Carrots:

Scrape 12 carrots and quarter them lengthwise. Melt 2 Tbl. butter in baking dish. Arrange carrots in dish. Sprinkle with ¼ c. minced onion, 1 tsp. salt, 1 tsp. sugar, and 4 tsp. ginger. Add 1/3 c. light cream or water. Cover and bake at 375 degrees for 30 minutes or until tender. Remove cover last 5 minutes. Watch so they don't burn and add more cream or water, heated, if necessary. Serves 4 to 6.

Turnip Puff:

Heat oven to 350 degrees. Peel and dice 6 to 8 medium white turnips. Cook, covered, in lightly salted water until tender. Drain and mash over low heat. Add 2 Tbl. butter or margarine, 1 tsp. salt, some pepper, 2 tsp. sugar, and ½ tsp. flour. Beat 2 egg yolks until light and gradually add to turnips. Beat 2 egg whites until stiff and fold into turnip mixture. Pour into greased 6 c. casserole. Bake 30 to 35 minutes until puffy and light brown.

Serve immediately to 4. Do not make ahead.

Fennel:

Remove any bruised parts from 4 large fennel bulbs. Cut whole bulb and any green part into small pieces. Bring 2 c. beef bouillon to boil and add fennel. Cover and cook slowly 20 minutes. Uncover. Add 1 Tbl. tomato paste or puree, pinch of sugar, salt and pepper to taste. Stir and let cook slowly several minutes.

Before serving to 4 or 6, add 3 Tbl. grated cheese. (Note: The 2 c. bouillon might be more than some would like to use.)

PORRIDGE
(The Age-old Method)

Oatmeal, like coffee, must be kept closely packed and air-tight. Quality, too, is important. Far too much oatmeal on the market is mass-milled by a process that injures both its flavor and its nutritive qualities, and far too many cooks not bred in the tradition steep it for hours on end, and eventually serve up a gluey, flavorless mess with sugar, and, to crown all, hot milk! But who that has tasted porridge properly made and served with cream or rich milk, will deny that it is food for the Gods?

Home-milled Meal   Salt   Fresh Spring Water

Allow for each person a breakfastcupful of water, a handful of oatmeal (about 1¼ oz.) of medium quality, and a small saltspoonful of salt. Put the water on in the porridge pot (it is advisable to keep a thick-bottomed pot exclusively for the porridge), and as soon as the water reaches boiling-point add the oatmeal, letting it fall in a steady rain from the left hand whilst you stir it with the right, using either a spurtle or the handle of a long wooden spoon. When the porridge is boiling steadily, draw it to the side, cover and cook gently. Cook for 10 minutes or so before adding salt. (If added before or along with the meal, it has a tendency to harden the grain.) Boil for 20-30 minutes in all, according to taste and the quality of the grain. (Some old farmers will not allow it to be boiled longer than 10 minutes.) Ladle into wooden bowls or cold soup plates, and serve with small individual bowls of cream or rich milk. Sup preferabley with a horn spoon (porridge is apt to over-heat a metal spoon), and dip each spoonful of porridge into the cold milk before conveying it to the mouth.

Perfect porridge requires a fourth ingredient -- hill or sea air!

Compliments of the Alma Chamber of Commerce, sponsor of the Alma Highland Festival and Games each spring.

BUTTERMILK BREAD

1 lb. flour	1 tsp. bicarbonate of soda
1 oz. sugar	1 tsp. cream of tartar
1 oz. butter	A pinch of salt
Buttermilk	

Sift the flour into a basin. Add the soda, cream of tartar, salt and sugar. Rub in the butter. (If good farmhouse buttermilk is used, the butter may be omitted.) Make into a soft dough with the milk. About half a pint should be enough. Put into a floured loaf tin and bake in a moderate oven for 45 minutes or till risen and firm.

*   *   *

STRAWBERRY SANDWICH
(Aberdeenshire)

3 oz. flour	1 c. strawberries
4 oz. sugar	1 gill double cream
1 tsp. baking powder	1 white of egg
1 Tbl. hot water	1½ oz. castor sugar
3 eggs	½ tsp. vanilla essence

Separate the yolks and whites of the eggs. Beat the whites stiffly. Add one yolk and beat three minutes; do the same with the second and the third; then add the sugar and water, and beat 5 minutes. Sift the flour and baking powder, and stir in lightly. Turn into two prepared sandwich tins and bake for twenty minutes in a fairly hot oven. Turn out and cool on a wire tray.

Mash the strawberries with a fork. Beat the egg white till stiff. Whisk the cream till quite thick, and fold in the egg white. Add the sugar and strawberries by degrees, and flavor with vanilla. Spread one cake with the filling, and place the other on top.

*   *   *

Detroit and U.P. Settlers

The first Italian to set foot in what is now Michigan was probably Henry de Tonti who, with Robert Cavelier de la Salle, explored the Great Lakes during the years 1678-79. Twenty-two years later in 1701 his brother, Alphonse de Tonti, landed at a site along the strait connecting Lake Erie and Lake St. Clair. In his position as second in command to Antoine de la Monthe Cadillac, Alphonse Tonti was one of the founders of the City of Detroit. Tonti's wife accompanied him to the wilderness outpost and their daughter, Teresa, became the first white child born in Michigan.

During the early decades of the nineteenth century a few Italians settled in the rapidly growing city of Detroit. Some may have come because of the political revolutions in Italy of 1848 or to seek a way out of the hard life in their native land. By 1855 the Italian community of Detroit included Gorgio Raggio, a Genoese who had a boarding house and an inn; Pasquale Palmieri, a Neapolitan artist; Mr. and Mrs. Cavari who kept a boarding house; Giovanni Arcetti from Genoa; Mr. Bozzevia Genoese; Mr. Mazzoli, a Tuscan statue maker; Francesco Cardoni, a native of Como, who made statues and imported monuments; and the Vitale Forni family from Genoa.

In the following years of the late nineteenth century many other Italians migrated to Detroit. In addition to Genoese, numbers of Lombards and Sicilians came to southeast Michigan. A group of Sicilian fruit merchants arrived in Detroit from Cleveland in 1883. By 1890 the census showed 338 native Italians in Detroit.

The formation of fraternal societies and religious organizations has always served as a mark of the growth of an ethnic community. As early as 1873 Detroit Italians had formed a mutual aid society and in 1889 the Lombard Society of Mutual Help set up headquarters in Detroit. By 1915 when the waves of southern European immigrants had reached the state a branch of the Sons of Italy was established in Michigan's bursting metropolis. Today the Detroit area boasts nearly 100 Italian organizations.

By Richard Hathaway

Detroit Italians had no church or priest until 1894 when Father J. Molinari arrived. In 1898 San Francesco Church was dedicated, and an Italian school began in 1902 led to the founding in 1910 of Holy Family Church. Not all Italians were Catholics. An Italian Evangelical Church was established in 1898 and Italian Presbyterian, Baptist and Methodist congregations were organized.

The last decade of the nineteenth century and the first twenty years of the twentieth were a period of heavy migration of Italians to the United States. By 1920 about 16,200 Italians had settled in Detroit. In 1909 an Italian language weekly newspaper *La Tribuna Italiano del Michigan* was begun to meet the needs of the growing community.

Many of the Italians who arrived in Detroit came to work in the stove and pharmaceutical companies; later they labored in the booming auto factories. However, traditional occupations such as fruit selling, grocery stores, food wholesaling, stone masons and restaurants attracted Italians. Today Italian-Americans are found in all areas of business, professions, the arts, educational and political endeavor.

In the early twentieth century many Italians settled on Detroit's east side, north of Fort Street and south of Gratiot. Another group lived between Six and Eight Mile Roads. Today there are approximately 250,000 Italian-Americans (about 97,000 Italian born) in southeast Michigan.

Detroit has not by any means been the only place in Michigan where Italians have migrated to, worked and settled. Another center of Italian-American life can be found far to the north in the western Upper Peninsula.

Beginning in the early 1870s Italian men, women and children arrived in the Upper Peninsula's Copper Country. Their experience in mining in Italy and the booming copper mines of Keweenaw and Houghton Counties drew them to the area. Many settled in Calumet, Ahmeek, Houghton and Laurium. Sili Lenzi came to Calumet in 1872 when he was 29 years old. He first found work as a miner with the Calumet and Hecla Mining Company but in 1878 opened a wine, liquor and cigar store. James Lisa, who came to Calumet as early as 1873, served for many years as Consul for the Italian government. The consular agent along with Calumet organizations such as the Italian Hall, the Cristoforo Columbo Band, the Italian Dramatic Club and the Garibaldi Club, helped Italian families adjust to life in the Copper Country. Italian miners in the town of Red Jacket, close by Calumet, formed the Italian Aid Society in 1874.

Many Italians such as Alfred Lazzeri, George Zeia, James Bonini, Dante Romanini and Angello Vangelisti worked at the famous old Quincy mine. These men with their countrymen and families made up the extensive Italian colony near Hancock. A Laurium newspaper *Minatore Italiana* (Italian Miner) stated that in 1910 over 3,500 Italians lived in the Copper Country. By 1900, 1894 Italian born immigrants lived in Houghton county. Wayne County, by contrast, was at that time home to but 937. Most Italians in the Copper Country worked the mines but some established stores or worked at the trades they brought with them.

The iron mines of the Upper Peninsula also attracted the Italian immigrant. The Marquette iron area became home to many Italians. The first Italian immigrants in Ishpeming came from the southern province of Calabria. Among the first was Bruno Nardi who owned a saloon. Another early Italian settler in Ishpeming was a shoemaker named Polito. One of the earliest Ishpeming grocery stores was founded by Dominic Andriacchi. The store is still today owned and operated by the family. In contrast to Ishpeming, the early Italian immigrants to Negaunee came from the northern section of Italy.

Despite the many Italians in the Copper Country and the Marquette area, the center of Italian culture in the Upper peninsula shifted to the Iron Mountain area on the Menominee Iron Range. The first Italians in Iron Mountain worshipped at the parish of Saint Joseph's. In 1889 Father Pelisson was assigned to St. Joseph's to care for the needs of the growing Italian community in the area. In the spring of 1890 the Italian community separated from St. Joseph's, purchased a lot in Gay's subdivision of Iron Mountain and built a frame church. Their pastor, Raphael Cavicchi, lived on the second floor. This church was named Holy Rosary and was the first Italian church in the Upper Peninsula. In 1893 the church burned and Father Cavicchi directed the re-building. This second structure was christened Assumption Church. April of 1902 brought Father Sinipli to this community of Italian miners in the far north. He immediately began the building of a new church. The miners, many of whom worked in the Chapin mine, donated their time to the construction. The stone for the walls was quarried locally. On December 8th, 1902 the church of Immaculate Conception Parish was dedicated. Although the parish opened its doors in 1942 to Catholics of all nationalities, the parish remains predominantly Italian up to today.

Many other areas in Michigan besides Detroit and the Upper Peninsula's mining regions have become home to Michigan Italians. The Giuffra and Cavagnaro families arrived in Grand Rapids before 1890. Soon thereafter families with the names of Casabianca, Caramella and Braccio immigrated to Michigan's western metropolis. As early as 1889 the Italians in Grand Rapids had formed a congregation which became Our Lady of Sorrows Church. These early Italian settlers in Grand Rapids found work in the plaster mines and the food business. Beginning in 1910 Italians from southern Italy came to Grand Rapids. This group settled in the area south of Wealthy Street, west of Jefferson to Ionia, and south to Hall Street. By 1920, 552 Italian immigrants lived in the Grand Rapids - Kent County area.

Italians began immigrating to Battle Creek shortly after the turn of the century. Alex Ratti came from Ann Arbor in 1906 to establish a soda fountain and ice cream parlor on West Main Street. A colony of Italians settled in Springfield Place and formed the Italian-American Brotherhood Club. In 1905 Tony Charameda came to Battle Creek where he went into the fruit and grocery business with Jim Tenuta.

Other cities in Michigan such as Pontiac, Lansing, Flint, Monroe, Wyandotte, Muskegon, Bay City, Ionia and Saginaw as well as the fruit growing areas (a type of farming familiar to many Italian immigrants) of southwestern Michigan have a sizeable population of Italian-Americans.

The heritage of Italian-Americans in Michigan is a proud one. The daughters and sons of Italian-American settlers plus recent immigrants continue to add their culture and skills to the productive and fascinating mixture which makes up the people of Michigan.

STEWED CHICKEN, HUNTER'S STYLE

1 chicken (about 3¼ lb.)	½-¾ lb. mushrooms, finely
½ c. olive oil	chopped or 1 1/3 oz. Italian
1 onion, chopped	dried mushrooms, soaked
1 carrot, chopped	in warm water 30 minutes
1 stalk celery, chopped	squeezed dry
2 Tbl. butter	Salt and pepper
¼ c. flour	2 c. dry white wine
½ lb. tomatoes, peeled	
and sliced	

Wash the chicken and cut in serving pieces. Heat the oil in a large skillet and saute the chopped onion, carrot and celery lightly. Add the pieces of chicken. Keep the heat high and turn the chicken gently with a wooden spoon until it is browned all over. Cream the butter and flour with a fork until it is smooth. Add this to the chicken together with the mushrooms, salt and pepper. Add in the wine and when this has evaporated, add the sliced tomatoes. When the mixture comes to a boil, cover and reduce the heat. Simmer for at least 1 hour, stirring occasionally. When the chicken is tender, correct the seasoning. Serve the chicken from a heated dish.

Corn meal mush (polenta) accompanied with a sauce of red and green peppers is often served with this dish.

*   *   *

By Mena Castriciano

RICOTTA CHEESECAKE

1 lb. ricotta or cottage cheese	½ c. all-purpose flour
½ c. sugar	1/3 c. golden seedles raisins
Grated rind of 1 lemon	½ c. candied fruit, finely chopped
4 egg yolks	2 egg whites

Sieve the ricotta or cottage cheese into a bowl. Work in the sugar and grated lemon rind. Add the egg yolks one at a time, then the flour, raisins and candied fruit. Beat the egg whites until stiff; fold them gently into the cheese mixture.

Butter a 9-inch round layer pan 2 inches deep and coat it with sugar and bread crumbs. Pour the cake mixture into the pan and bake in a preheated 350 degree oven for about 30 minutes.

When ready, remove the cake from the oven. Let it cool. Then turn it out onto a serving plate.

*   *   *

VERMICELLI WITH HAM AND PEAS

4 Tbl. butter	½ c. stock
1/8 lb. boiled ham, diced	Salt
¼ c. chopped onion	1 c. dry white wine
1 lb. peas, shelled	1 lb. vermicelli
Pinch sugar	1 c. grated Parmesan cheese
Pepper	

Put the butter, the fattest part of the ham and the chopped onion in a saucepan. Cook over low heat so that the onion does not brown. Add the peas, sugar, a little pepper and the stock. Raise the heat to high and boil the mixture, stirring constantly, to cook the peas quickly. When the peas are almost tender, add the salt, wine and the remaining lean ham. Reduce the wine over high heat, then remove the pan and keep the contents warm. Cook the vermicelli in plenty of boiling salted water. Cook until firm to the bite. Drain and turn out onto bright plates. Toss with the ham and peas mixture. Serve accompanied with grated Parmesan cheese.

STUFFED TOMATOES

6 ripe tomatoes	Chopped basil
Salt	6 Tbl. olive oil
Chopped parsley	Pepper
1 clove garlic - chopped	6 slices Fontina cheese
(inner bud removed)	

Choose tomatoes of the same size. Wash them well, cut off the tops and, using a teaspoon, remove the seeds, pulp and juice. Lightly salt the insides and leave them standing upside down on a rack to drain the insides completely.

Prepare a stuffing of parsley, basil and garlic and season with oil and pepper. (Do not use salt, as the tomatoes have already been salted.) Fill the tomatoes with this mixture.

Place them closely together, but not touching, in a greased oven-proof dish in a preheated 450 degree oven for about 5 minutes. At the end of this time put a slice of Fontina cheese on each tomato; leave them in the oven for another 10 minutes. Serve hot, garnish with basil leaves and parsley sprigs.

      *   *   *

The Bois Blanc Sugar Camp

The following passages are from "Reminiscenses of Early Days in Mackinac Island", written by Elizabeth Therese Baird about her childhood days on the island in the early 1800s. Mrs. Baird, who moved to Wisconsin in later years, was the daughter of a Scottish fur trader and granddaughter of an Ottawa chief. She was also of French ancestry, as can be seen from these passages.

A visit to the sugar camp was a great treat to the young folks as well as the old. In the days I write of, sugar was a scarce article. All who were able possessed a sugar camp. My grandmother had one on Bois Blanc Island, about five miles east of Mackinac. About the first of March, nearly half the inhabitants of our town, as well as many from the garrison, would move to Bois Blanc to perpare for the work. Our camp was delightfully situated in the midst of a maple grove. A thousand or more trees claimed our care, and three men and two women were employed to do the work.

The "camp" was made of pole or small trees enclosed with sheets of cedar bark and was about thiry feet long by eighteen feet wide. On each side was a platform about eighteen inches high and four feet wide. One side was intended for beds, and each bed, when not in use, was rolled up nicely, wrapped in an Indian mat, then placed back against the wall; the bedroom became a sitting room. The walls on the inside were covered with tarpaulin, also the floor. The women's bedding was placed at one end of the platform. The platform on the opposite side served as a dining floor, one end of which was enclosed in cedar bark, forming a closet for the dishes and cooking utensils. The dishes consisted of some crockery, tin plates and cups, and wooden dishes and ladles. A wing was added at one end for the men's bedroom.

At either end of the camp were doors made large to admit heavy logs for the fire. The fireplace was midway between the two platforms and extended to within six feet of the doors. At each corner of the fireplace were large posts firmly planted in the ground and extending upwards about five feet or more. Large timbers were placed lengthwise on top of these posts, and across the timbers extended bars from which, by chains and hoops, were suspended large brass kettles, two on each bar. On the dining room side, half-way up the wall, ran a pole, horizontally. This was to hold in place hemlock branches which were brought in fresh every evening. The place between the fire and platforms was kept very neat by a thick, heavy broom made of cedar branches cut off evenly on the bottom, and with a long handle.

The hanging of the kettle was quite a test of skill requiring three persons to perform the task. The fire had to be burning briskly when the hanging began. It was the duty of one person to hang the kettle properly; of the second to immediately pour a small quantity of sap to keep the vessel from burning; of the third to fill it with the sap. The peak of the roof was left open to allow the smoke to escape -- and at night to let in the stars, as was my childish fancy. In early morning, the birds would arouse us to listen to their songs and catch a sight of the waning stars. Blue jays were especially numerous and so tame one could fairly enjoy them. Other birds would in turn sing and whistle as the stars disappeared and the day dawned. An owl made its abiding-place in a tree nearby, sentinel-like and ever-uttered its coo-coo-coo-hoo, as the Indian had named its sound. The sound of the whip-poor-will was a harbinger of spring and a warning that the time to cease sugar-making had arrived.

Now for the work. All the utensils used in making sugar were of that daintiest of material, birchbark. The "casseau" to set at the tree to catch the sap was a birchbark dish, holding from one to two gallons. The pails for carrying the sap were of the same material and held from three to four gallons. The men placed a "gauje", or yoke, on their shoulders, then a bucket would be suspended on each side. The women seldom used this yoke but assisted the men in carrying the buckets, doing so in the usual manner. The mocock in which the sugar was packed was also of birchbark and held from thirty to eighty pounds. The bark was gathered in the summer at Bark Point. The name was afterward done into French as "Point aux Ecorces." The sailors now miscall it "Point au Barques."

The "gouttiere," or spout, which was made of basswood, had to be cleaned each spring before it was placed in the tree. The birch-bark for the casseau was cleaned by taking off a layer of the inner bark and then washing it. The buckets were made by sewing the seams with bast, which is taken from the inner bark of basswood, then gummed over with pine pitch. They also were carefully washed and dried before use. As a matter of course, the larger vessels to receive

179

the sap were barrels made of oak. No pine was ever used about the camp as that would impart a disagreeable taste. The strainers were made of a particular kind of flannel of very coarse thread and not woolly, bought especially for this purpose by the merchants. I remember well the cleaning of these. After they had been used they were put into a tub of very hot water and washed (without soap) or pounded with a "battoir," or beetle, then rinsed in many waters.

By this time the sap must be boiling. It takes over four hours to make sap into syrup and the boiling is usually begun in the morning. The fire is kept bright all day and night. Two women are detailed to watch the kettles closely for when the sap boils down nearly to syrup it is liable to bubble over at any moment. The women therefore stand by with a branch of hemlock in hand. As the liquid threatens to boil over, they dip the branch in quickly, and, it being cool, the syrup is settled for a while. When at this stage, it requires closest watching. When the sap has boiled down about one-half, the women have to transfer the contents of one kettle to another, as the kettles must be kept full for fear of scorching the top of the kettle, which would spoil all. As fast as a kettle is emptied it will be filled with water and set aside, awaiting the general cleaning. The kettles require the utmost care, being scoured as soon as possible each time emptied, keeping one woman employed nearly all the time. Sand and water are the cleansing agents used.

All this time, if the weather favors the running of the sap, it is brought as fast as possible and the boiling goes on. At this period, my grandmother would send me my little barrel full of the syrup. This miniature barrel bears the date 1815 and is now dark and polished with age, and is a rare momento of those halcyon days. It holds less than a pint and was made by an Ottawa Indian out of a solid piece of wood, sides and ends all one, the interior being ingeniously burned out through the bung-hole. The receipt of this was the signal that the time had come when I too might visit the camp.

When made, the syrup is placed in barrels awaiting the time when it can be made into sugar of various kinds, the modus operandi is thus; a very bright brass kettle is placed over a slow fire (it cannot be done at boiling time, as then a brisk fire is required), this kettle containing about three gallons of syrup if it is to be made into cakes - if into "cassonade," or granulated sugar, two gallons of syrup are used. For the sugar cakes, a board of basswood is prepared about five or six inches wide with molds gouged in the form of bears, diamonds, crosses, rabbits, turtles, spheres, etc. When the sugar is cooked to a certain degree, it is poured into these molds. For the granulated sugar, the stirring is continued for a longer time, this being done with a long paddle which looks like a mushstick. This sugar has to be put into the mocock while warm, as it will not pack well if cold. This work is especially difficult; only a little can be made at a time, and it was always done under my grandmother's supervision.

The sugar-gum, or wax, is also made separately. Large wooden bowls, or birchbark casseaus, are filled with snow, and when the syrup is of the right consistency it is poured upon the snow in thin sheets. When cooled it is put into thin birchbark, made into a neat package, and tied with bast. The syrup made for table use is boiled very thick, which prevents its souring. For summer use, it is put into jugs and buried in the ground two or three feet deep where it will keep a year, more or less. The trip to Bois Blanc I made in my dog-sled. Francois Lacroix, the son of a slave, whom my grandmother reared, was my companion. The ride over the ice, across the lake, was a delightful one; the drive through the woods (which was notably clear of underbrush) to the camp, about a mile from shore, was equally charming.

The pleasures of the camp were varied. In out-of-door amusement, I found delight in playing about great trees that had been uprooted in some wind storm. Frequently, each season near the close of sugarmaking, parties of ladies and gentlemen would come over from Mackinac bent on a merry time, which they never failed to secure.

One time a party of five ladies and five gentlemen were invited to the camp. Each lady brought a frying pan in which to cook and turn "les crepes," or pancakes, which was to be the special feature and fun of the occasion. All due preparation was made for using the frying pan. We were notified that no girl was fit to be married until she could turn a crepe. Naturally all were desirous to try their skill in that direction whether matrimonially inclined or not. The gentlemen of the party tried their hand at it as well as the ladies. It may not be amiss here to explain what to turn the crepe meant; when the cake was cooked on one side, it was dexterously tossed in the air and expected to land, the other side up, back in the pan. Never did I see objects miss so widely the mark aimed at. It seemed indeed that the crepes were influenced by the glee of the party; they turned and flew everywhere but where wanted. Many fell into the fire as if the turner had so intended. Some went to the ground, and one even found its way to the platform over the head of the turner.

In due time a nice dinner was prepared. We had partridges roasted on sticks before the fire; rabbit and stuffed squirrel, cooked French fashion; and finally had as many crepes, with syrup, as we desired. Everyone departed with a bark of wax, or sugar cakes.

ONION SOUP

6 medium onions,
   sliced thin
6 Tbl. butter
1 tsp. salt
Dash nutmeg
6 c. beef stock

¼ c. sherry
6 thick slices, French
   bread
Grated Swiss and
   Parmesan cheese

Saute onion in butter until soft. Add salt and nutmeg. Cook until onions are golden brown. Add stock and bring to boil. Reduce heat and simmer 10 minutes. Add wine. Place soup into 6 soup cassroles and top with a piece of bread. Top with a thick layer of cheese. Bake at 300 degrees for 10 minutes. Serves 6.

*   *   *

PEA SOUP

2 c. dried yellow peas
Water
2 qts. cold water
½ lb. bacon, cut up
1 onion, minced

½ c. minced celery
2 carrots, chopped
¼ c. minced parsley
Salt and pepper
½ tsp. allspice

Soak peas overnight in water. Boil for 10 minutes in water to cover. Drain and discard water. Place peas in deep kettle. Add cold water, bacon, vegetables, and spices. Simmer, covered, over low heat 2-3 hours.

*   *   *

COQ AU VIN

3 Tbl. butter	½ lb. bacon, cut up
¾ c. chopped onions	3 shallots, minced
1 carrot, sliced	1 garlic clove
	1 frying chicken, cut up

Brown all ingredients, except chicken, together in a Dutch oven. Place to the side and brown chicken. Stir in:

2 Tbl. flour	½ tsp. thyme
2 Tbl. minced parsley	1 tsp. salt
1 Tbl. marjoram	Ground pepper
1 bay leaf	1 Tbl. brandy

Bring all ingredients to a simmer, then stir in 1½ c. dry red wine. Cover and simmer for 1 hour. Add ½ lb. mushrooms, if desired. Cover and cook 5 more minutes. Correct seasoning.

Serve chicken on a hot platter with the sauce and vegetables poured over it.

* * *

ARTICHOKE HEARTS AND PEAS

2 pkg. frozen artichoke hearts	2 Tbl. butter
4 Tbl. butter	¼ tsp. thyme
4 c. green peas	Pinch sugar
1 c. water	Salt and pepper

Thaw artichokes. Cut in half lengthwise and pat dry with a paper towel. Saute them in 4 Tbl. butter until lightly colored. Add remaining ingredients. Cover and simmer about 25 minutes, or until the peas are tender and the liquid has almost evaporated. Serves 8.

* * *

QUICHE LORRAINE

9-inch unbaked pie shell	1½ c. evaporated milk
½ lb. sliced bacon	1 tsp. salt
1½ c. grated Swiss cheese	Nutmeg
3 eggs	Pepper

Fry bacon until crisp. Drain on paper towels. Crumble on bottom of pie shell. Sprinkle with cheese.

Beat together remaining ingredients, tasting to correct seasonings. Pour into pie shell. Bake at 375 degrees 35-45 minutes, or until the top is golden and the center is firm. Cool on wire rack 10 minutes before serving.

*   *   *

FRENCH CREPES

Beat 2 eggs, ¾ c. milk, ½ c. plus 1 Tbl. flour, 1 tsp. oil and a pinch of salt. (For dessert crepes, add 2 tsp. sugar.) When smooth, let batter stand 1 hour before using.

Heat a frying pan and grease it with a few drops of oil and 1/8 tsp. butter for each crepe. Pour in 2-2½ Tbl. batter for each crepe. Cook over medium heat until bottom is lightly browned and the top is dry. Turn and brown the other side.

Roll them around a stuffing of chicken or seafood. For dessert, fill with jelly or fruit preserves, roll and sprinkle with powdered sugar. (Crepes can be covered with waxed paper and a towel and stored in the refrigerator for later use.)

*   *   *

CREPES SUZETTES

For a simple but elegant dessert, melt ½ c. butter and ½ c. orange marmalade in a chafing dish. Add ½ c. brandy, stirring well. Place crepes in mixture, folding into quarters and arranging in the sauce. When heated through, sprinkle with a little warm brandy. Ignite the sauce and serve flaming on heated plates.

*　　　　*　　　　*

CHOCOLATE MOUSSE

½ lb. bittersweet chocolate	5 egg yolks
	1 tsp. rum
¼ c. water	5 egg whites

In top of double boiler, over simmering water, mix chocolate and water. Stir until melted, then set aside to cool. Beat together 5 egg yolks and 1 tsp. rum. Add to chocolate. Beat egg whites until stiff. Fold into chocolate mixture. Pour into individual pots de creme or ramekins. Chill at least 2 hours. Serves 6-8.

*　　　　*　　　　*

MADELEINES

4 eggs	½ c. melted butter
½ c. sugar	Grated rind of 1 lemon
1 1/8 c. flour	

In top of double boiler, over simmering water, beat eggs and sugar with wooden spoon until creamy and lukewarm. Take from heat and beat again until cold. Beat in flour, butter and rind. Butter and flour shell-shaped Madeleine molds. Fill 2/3 full of batter. Bake at 400 degrees for 25 minutes. Makes about 12.

Index

Salads

Breads, Pancakes, Dumplings

Main Dishes

Vegetables

Cookies, Cakes, Pastries

Desserts

About the Editor

CAROLE EBERLY is a former legislative reporter for United Press International. A freelance writer and editor, she is also a faculty member at Michigan State University's School of Journalism. Besides cooking and eating, Carole's pasttimes include running, going to the movies, playing with her five cats, finding great bargains at various stores and lazing around a log cabin (with a great fireplace and no telephone) in Northern Michigan.

Other Eberly Press Books:

Brownie Recipes. Cream cheese brownie supreme, blast-me-to-heaven chocolate chip coconut bars..and 170 more. Throw out your bathroom scale, move your waistband over an inch. $7.95

Christmas in Michigan: Tales and Recipes. Celebrate Christmas on Mackinac Island in the 1800s with a young French woman. Relive Christmas in Detroit when streetcars took you gift shopping. Travel to the U.P. during the Depression when food was scarce, but not the Christmas spirit. Re-enter the kitchen of your grandmothers to smell and taste their cookies, cakes and Christmas puddings. $7.95

Michigan Summers: Tales and Recipes. Relive a 1950s trip to Mackinaw City on the old roads. Visit a one-ring circus in the 1860s. Travel to a Lake Michigan island where Nature has forbidden any human to inhabit. Michigan summertime photos from long ago to the present. Create your own Michigan meals with blueberry soup, spinach cheese squares, strawberry pudding...and more. $7.95

Please enclose $2 for postage and handling of two books or less; $3 for three books or more.

Eberly Press
1004 Michigan Ave.
E. Lansing, MI 48823